Sixty-One Gospel Talks for Children

Sixty-One
GOSPEL TALKS
for Children

BY ELDON WEISHEIT

CONCORDIA
PUBLISHING HOUSE

Bible quotations are from the Revised Standard Version, copyright 1946 and 1952, by the Division of Christian Education of the National Council of Churches, and are used by permission.

ISBN 0-570-03204-0

Concordia Publishing House, St. Louis, Missouri
© 1969 Concordia Publishing House

Library of Congress Catalog Card No. 70-96217

MANUFACTURED IN THE UNITED STATES OF AMERICA

10 11 12 13 14 15 16 17 18 CB 89 88 87 86 85 84 83

To my parents,
Harry and Edna Weisheit

Contents

Preface	9
Yell for the Right Kind of Help	11
Two Kinds of Signs	13
The Right Gift for the Right Person	15
Test the Christmas Lights	17
It's the Gift That Counts	19
Is Christ in the "Cast of Characters" of Your Life?	21
You Don't Have a "Toy Savior"	23
The Kind of Help That God Gives	25
Why Follow the Star?	27
Do You Know Where to Look?	29
It's Easy If You Know How	31
How Far Can You Trust Jesus?	33
When Will You Ask for Help?	35
Saved for a Reason	37
A Beautiful Sight — Seen Through a Mess	39
All This and Heaven Too	41
Directions Are for Following	43
Take a Long-Range View	45
Don't Be Tempted Alone	47
A Lot of a Little — Or a Little of a Lot	49
Keep Your Life in Balance	51
Do You Know How to Use a Gift?	53
What You Don't Know Can Hurt You	55
In the Yellow Pages — Under "Savior"	57
It Is Finished	59
After the End Comes the Beginning	61
Seeing Is Not Believing	63
The Shepherd Who Leads	65
Sorrow That Brings Joy	67
Help That Stays — By Going Away	69

Pray in His Name	71
Who Makes the Rules?	73
How Well Can You Remember?	75
A New Creation from an Old One	77
Read the Instructions First	79
Make Your Choice	81
Who Is the Most Important?	83
You Can't Give Until You Get	85
Don't Forget the Lure	87
How Good Do I Have to Be?	89
You Can Afford to Care	91
Watch What You Eat	93
How to Be on the Winning Team	95
It's a Crying Shame	97
Life Is an Open Book	99
Wait for the Whole Story	101
I Didn't Do Anything Wrong	103
Receive the Gift and the Giver	105
Don't Follow "Shortcut" Religion	107
Choose Your Lifesaver	109
Be Yourself	111
Look at Both Sides	113
You Can Check the Power	115
Accept the Invitation You Receive	117
Whom Can You Trust?	119
The Forgiven Are Forgiving	121
Where Does Your Money Go?	123
How to Do a Miracle	125
Treasure in a Junkpile	127
Jesus in Everyday Life	129
When Will You Get Ready?	131

Preface

No one ever accused Jesus of living in an ivory tower or of being irrelevant or of avoiding an issue. His ministry was on the level of the people He ministered to. He did not give lectures on public health problems, but He was on the scene with the sick and the crippled. He healed many and often used the healing as a way to reach through a man's body into his soul. He faced death without the pious platitudes that men of all ages have used to have something to say about a subject they know nothing about. Instead He restored life and endured death Himself. He discussed guilt with those who knew they were guilty, and offered them holiness. He discussed holiness with those who thought they were holy and exposed their guilt. He was involved in the social problem of prejudice against Samaritans and the political problem of Roman rule.

All these things are recorded in the Gospels. Gospel means "good news." But as we read the Gospels to fight their battles and to share their victories, they often come out as "good history." The heroic story of God entering human flesh to take all of man's suffering upon Himself happened 1,900 years ago. The ultimate victory of resurrection has resulted in many monuments and many speeches to celebrate the victory. But where is the life that it gives?

The worship talks in this book are based on texts from the Gospels. They are also based on the belief that the Gospel is good news. They hold to a faith that says Christ did not ascend into an ivory tower. Christ did not speak to a page of history but to all history. Christ still ministers to people through those who proclaim His Word and those who live His Word. These talks are proclamations of a Christ who lives today. As Christ used stories and objects from His time on earth to illustrate His message, so objects from today's world are used to illustrate the same message.

These messages are addressed to children, but they are intended not only for the child who is yet a child but also for the child who has become a man. Children are often expected to sit through worship services planned for and by adults and delivered by and to adults. To the child it is an alien world. He has never been an adult and wonders if he ever wants to become one. But the adult has been a child. What man can ever forget the joy of a home run or the disappointment of a strikeout? What woman does not remember when she first used her mother's real iron? What adult doesn't still like to play with balloons, receive gifts, talk about magic?

My thanks to the members of The Lutheran Church of the Epiphany, Montgomery, Ala., for their kind response to these messages. Also thanks to my wife Carolyn and to my sons Dirk, Tim, and Wes for always being willing to collect the objects needed to illustrate these sermons. And thanks to our gracious God for giving me a job that allows me, and at times even forces me, to work so closely with His Word.

ELDON WEISHEIT

Yell for the Right Kind of Help

The Word

The crowds that went before Him and that followed Him shouted: "Blessed is He who comes in the name of the Lord! Hosanna in the highest!" And when He entered Jerusalem, all the city was stirred, saying, "Who is this?" And the crowds said: "This is the prophet Jesus from Nazareth of Galilee." Matthew 21:9-11 (from the Gospel for the First Sunday in Advent)

The World

A large, opened tin can with the lid still attached, a red marker pencil, a small first-aid kit.

Do you know what to do when you are in trouble? One answer that applies to almost every need is to yell for help. The people in our text yelled for help. They called out, "Hosanna!" which means, "Help us!" As we prepare to celebrate the birth of Christ, we also call out to Jesus, saying, "Hosanna!" or "Help us!" Let's look at another situation when you might have to yell for help and from it learn when we can ask Christ for help.

Suppose you were out playing in an empty lot and found a tin can like this one. You decide that you could use it for something, but as you are trying to twist off the lid, you cut yourself. I won't really cut myself, because I know that it would hurt, but I will mark my finger with this red pencil to make it look like it is bleeding. If you were really out alone and were cut, you would have to yell for help.

But the first person who hears your yell for help and comes takes one look at the tin can and says: "You shouldn't have been playing with that tin can. Shame on you! Don't

11

you know any better?" Then he walks away. That did not help you any. You already knew that you had done something wrong. So you have to yell again.

Another person comes. He looks at your finger and says: "You have a serious cut on your right finger. There is danger of infection. You had also better be careful not to lose too much blood." He also leaves. He didn't help you any by telling you how serious the cut was. So you yell again.

The third person to come sees your cut and runs back to his car. He returns with a first-aid kit. Then he quickly cleans the cut and protects it with a Band-Aid.

That was a pretend story. But all of us have a problem that is not pretend. We have sinned against God. In many different ways we have broken His commandments. It is a real problem. We need help. So we yell for help. We cry, "Hosanna!"

But we have to know to whom we are yelling for help. It would not help our problem of sin for someone to tell us how bad our sins are. It would not help for someone to tell us what punishment we will receive for our sins. When we cry, "Help us!" we need someone who can solve the problem of sin.

That is why we ask Christ to help us. He is the One who came to earth. He saw our problem, and He died for our sins. But He returned by His resurrection from the dead to give us a victory over sin.

During these weeks of Advent we think of our sins to understand why Jesus came. But as we think of them we do not have to be afraid. We can yell for help. We can say, "Hosanna, Jesus!" and He answers our prayer by coming to us also.

Two Kinds of Signs

The Word

There will be signs in sun and moon and stars, and upon the earth distress of nations in perplexity at the roaring of the sea and the waves, men fainting with fear and with foreboding of what is coming on the world; for the powers of the heavens will be shaken. And then they will see the Son of Man coming in a cloud with power and great glory. Now when these things begin to take place, look up and raise your heads, because your redemption is drawing near. Luke 21:25-28 (from the Gospel for the Second Sunday in Advent)

The World

Two sets of signs: one showing miles to a nearby city, e. g., "Birmingham 50 miles," "Birmingham 30 miles," "Birmingham 15 miles"; the other advertising events in the same city, e. g., "Climb the Iron Man in Birmingham," "Save at Birmingham National Bank," "Visit the Birmingham Zoo."

Suppose that your family is out driving and gets lost. You will probably watch for road signs that tell you where you are. When you come to a large highway and see this sign (show "Birmingham 50 miles"), it tells you two things: first, which city the road leads to, and second, how far away it is. If you follow that road, you will continue to see signs like these (show "Birmingham 30 miles," "Birmingham 15 miles"). Each sign tells you that you are on the right road and that you are getting nearer to the city.

There are also other signs that help you if you are lost. If you are driving down a highway and see this sign (show "Climb the Iron Man in Birmingham"), you know the road leads to Birmingham. The sign tells you which way you are going, but it does not tell you how far you have to go. As you drive down the highway, you will see other signs like these (show "Save at Birmingham National Bank," and "Visit the Birmingham Zoo"), advertising things to do in Birmingham. Each sign is an assurance that you are on the right road, but none of them tells you how far away the city is.

Jesus holds up some signs for us to see in our text. He says there will be signs in sun and moon and stars. He reminds us that distress among nations is a sign. He tells us that men will be afraid and that the powers of the earth will be shaken. These things are signs that Christ will return to the earth in power and great glory on Judgment Day.

These signs from Jesus are like the second set of signs I showed you. They tell you where you are going but not how far away the destination is. We do not read the signs to figure out when the end of the world is coming. Only God knows when the Day will be, but each generation receives signs to remind them that the Day is coming.

The signs that Jesus shows describe things that often make people afraid. But if we see them as signs of Christ's coming, we need not be afraid. Instead the signs give us comfort. We live in a world that has many problems. Each sign describes a problem. But God knows about our problems. Christ has come to be our Savior. God has given us help in living with these problems. He has told us that they will not destroy us but we shall receive a victory when Christ comes in His power and great glory.

Each time you see or hear about any of the signs that Jesus mentioned, you will be reminded that He is coming to take you to be with Him in heaven.

The Right Gift for the Right Person

The Word

Now when John heard in prison about the deeds of the Christ, he sent word by his disciples and said to Him: "Are you He who is to come, or shall we look for another?" And Jesus answered them: "Go and tell John what you hear and see: the blind receive their sight and the lame walk, lepers are cleansed and the deaf hear, and the dead are raised up, and the poor have good news preached to them." Matthew 11:2-5 (from the Gospel for the Third Sunday in Advent)

The World

Three Christmas packages about the same size and shape, representing, though not necessarily containing, a bottle of perfume, a fountain pen, and a pocketknife.

Here are three Christmas gifts, all wrapped and ready for you to give to your family. One is a bottle of perfume for your mother. Another is a fountain pen for your father. The third is a pocketknife for your brother. Since the gifts were wrapped at the store, all you have to do is put them under the tree and wait for Christmas.

But wait! Which package has the pocketknife? Which one is the perfume? The gifts are all about the same size, shape, and weight. There are no tags on the packages. It would be embarrassing to give your father or brother perfume. And your mother wouldn't want a pocketknife. To avoid having a mix-up on Christmas, we had better check the packages. By opening just one end, I can see that this is the perfume; so it can be labeled TO MOTHER. This one is the pocketknife, which means the other one would have to be the fountain pen. Now you can give the right gift to the right person.

In the story of our text John the Baptizer thought he was getting the wrong gift. He had done his job, which was to tell people to prepare for Christ's coming. He had clearly pointed to Jesus and said, "Behold the Lamb of God, who takes away the sin of the world." But then look what happened. He was arrested and thrown into jail. It seemed like someone got the packages mixed up. Surely a servant of God would not be thrown into jail! So John sent two disciples to ask Jesus if He really was the Messiah.

Jesus answered by saying: "Go and tell John what you hear and see: the blind receive their sight and the lame walk, lepers are cleansed and the deaf hear, and the dead are raised up, and the poor have good news preached to them." Jesus had the right gift for each person. The blind received sight, the deaf could hear, the lame could walk again. But Jesus' gifts were not limited to healing the sick. For some who died He offered a resurrection—a return to life. But even the gift of a resurrection from the dead was not His greatest gift. He also had good news for the poor. He had the good news that His help was greater than healing the sick or even returning a man to life on this earth. He offered the good news that the guilt of sin could be removed and man could live forever with God.

This was the good news for John in prison. It was also the good news for the blind who did not receive their sight and the deaf who did not have their hearing restored.

We often do not understand the gifts of God. It is impossible to understand if we look only at the gifts that we receive on this earth. But if we think that the greatest gift is something more than health, money, or honor, if the greatest gift was the gift of God's Son to be our Savior, then we know God has given the right gift. And the right gift has come to the right person when you receive it.

Test the Christmas Lights

The Word

And this is the testimony of John, when the Jews sent priests and Levites from Jerusalem to ask him, "Who are you?" He confessed, he did not deny, but confessed, "I am not the Christ." And they asked him, "What then? Are you Elijah?" He said, "I am not." "Are you the prophet?" And he answered, "No." They said to him then, "Who are you? Let us have an answer for those who sent us. What do you say about yourself?" He said: "I am the voice of one crying in the wilderness, 'Make straight the way of the Lord,' as the prophet Isaiah said." John 1:19-23 (from the Gospel for the Fourth Sunday in Advent)

The World

A string of Christmas tree lights and a handful of bulbs — some burned out and some good.

Putting up the Christmas tree is a part of getting ready for Christmas. Most of you probably have lights like these on your Christmas tree. We use lights at Christmas to show that Christ, who is the Light of the world, has come into the world, which is filled with the darkness of sin. We call these "Christmas lights" (hold up bulbs), but sometimes they don't make light. Each year when you get out your Christmas decorations, some lights are burned out. If you want to have light on your Christmas tree, you have to remove the ones that don't work and replace them with new bulbs.

That means you have to test each bulb by screwing it into the socket. See, this one works, so we'll keep it. This one doesn't, so we'll throw it away. And so on. We can test all these bulbs.

In our text some religious leaders are testing John the

Baptizer in a way similar to the way I tested the light bulbs. They ask him if he is the Christ. He says that he is not. They wonder if he is Elijah returned to earth, or the prophet. To each question John says, "No." Then John tells them who he is. He is the one who was to prepare the way for Christ. When it came to the subject of the coming of Christ to earth, John's light went on. This was his job. This gave him his purpose in living.

Just as John was to prepare the world for Christmas, so we also prepare for Christmas. We give and receive gifts, have parties, send Christmas cards, sing Christmas songs, have special foods. But how many of these things help you see Christmas as the coming of Christ into the world? Do you do these things because others do them or because you think you have to? or because they really help you understand the birth of Christ?

Pretend that each of the Christmas practices you follow is a light bulb like these. Now check your practice to see if it works. Does buying gifts make you happy to share with others? Is it a way of showing the love Christ has given you? Then it is a Christmas light that works. Continue to give presents. Or does it make you unhappy to spend money for gifts and cards? Do you give gifts because you have to? Then your giving is not a Christmas light. Throw it out. Do Christmas parties make you happy? Can you feel the joy of sharing Christ with others? Or do you gripe because you don't win the prize? Does receiving gifts make you thankful, or do they make you wonder why you didn't receive more?

Talk these things over with your family. Then plan a Christmas that is filled with lights that work — lights that show the love of Christ to you and to others.

It's the Gift That Counts

The Word

For to you is born this day in the city of David a Savior, who is Christ the Lord. And this will be a sign for you: you will find a babe wrapped in swaddling cloths and lying in a manger. Luke 2:11-12 (from the Gospel for Christmas Day)

The World

A beautifully wrapped box that contains nothing, and a sack from a store that contains an expensive gift, such as a watch.

If these two packages were under your Christmas tree and you were told to choose one, which would you take? This one looks more like a gift. It is beautifully wrapped. It would probably catch your eye first. But if you chose it, you would be disappointed. (Unwrap the gift.) See, this was only a box wrapped to look like a gift. It was used only for display purposes and wasn't really a gift at all.

This other package has a real gift in it. Though the wrapping is only a paper sack, it contains this beautiful watch. If you would have received this watch for Christmas, you would have been so happy about the gift that you would not have cared about the wrapping. It is the gift that counts — not the package it comes in.

This is also true of God's gift to you. Our text tells the story of God's gift to all people. God sent His Son to be our Savior. The angel told the shepherds they would find this great gift wrapped in swaddling cloths and lying in a manger. Swaddling cloths were not rags in the sense of old clothes.

19

All babies born then were wrapped tightly in long bands of cloth, called swaddling cloths, to give them straight backs.

The fact that Jesus was wrapped in swaddling cloths made Him no different from any other baby. But He was also lying in a manger — a cheap nursery for the Son of God who was to be the Savior of the world. It might have been more impressive for Jesus to have been born in a big palace with many attendants. Maybe He should have had a satin-lined crib and blankets with gold and silver decorations.

But Jesus was such a great gift to the world that He did not need the outward appearance of greatness that the world gives. He could prove His greatness not by copying our attempts at showing greatness but by giving us something far greater than any man could achieve. He showed His greatness by His ability to love all people and by His death and resurrection, which destroyed the power of sin.

As we receive the gift of God's Son today, let us never confuse the wrappings with the gift. The importance of your baptism does not depend on whether or not you had a long baptismal dress. It makes no difference whether you were baptized in a beautiful church or a lonely hospital room. These things are only the wrappings. The gift of baptism is a new birth in Jesus Christ.

When you come to worship, remember the gift you receive. You receive the love of Christ. God gives you forgiveness for all your sins. You are given the privilege of praising God and asking for His help. The music, the church building, the candles and beautiful church furniture are all nice to have. But they are only wrappings. If they help you appreciate the gift of Christ, they have served their purpose. But if they become attractions in themselves, then you are confusing the wrappings with the gift.

God has chosen the gift for you. He gives you Christ today. It's the gift that counts.

Is Christ in the "Cast of Characters" of Your Life?

The Word

Simeon blessed them and said to Mary His mother: "Behold, this Child is set for the fall and rising of many in Israel." Luke 2:34 (from the Gospel for the Sunday After Christmas)

The World

A balloon, a pin, a nut.

Most stories have two parts. One part is about conflict or trouble. It is the part of the story that makes you worry or cry. It is the sad part of the story. The other part of a story is the success part. It is the part that makes you happy. It tells how the good guy wins. A story has a happy ending if the conflict comes first and then the success. A story has a sad ending when the success comes first and then the conflict.

For example, the story of a balloon starts with success. See, I blow it up. The balloon now serves its purpose. It adds a bit of happiness to a party. Then the balloon is broken. That's the end of the story, because that's the end of the balloon. It is a sad ending.

Now let's have an example of the other kind of story. See this nut. You are used to eating nuts. But they are also seeds. If you put this seed into the ground, it would appear to rot. That would be the sad part of the story. But if you could watch the seed under the ground, you would see something else happen. Though it at first appeared to be dead, you would see it come to life by sending out a little shoot, which would eventually grow into a tree. This story had the sad part first, but it changed to a happy story because the seed grew to become a tree.

Our lives also have either happy or sad endings — depending on how we look at life. In our text Simeon points to the baby Jesus and says that He is "set for the fall and rising of many in Israel." Notice that he said "fall and rising," not "rising and fall." Often we look at life as rising and fall; that is, we work and plan throughout our lives to achieve great things. That is the rising. Then comes old age, sickness, and death. That is the fall. This view of life makes it a sad story.

But when Jesus is in your life, the story is the other way around. First there is a fall. The presence of Christ reminds us of our sins. His coming shows that the world needs a Savior. It tells us that the wages of sin is death. That is the unhappy part of the story. But it is better to have that part of the story first. Do not ignore your need for a Savior. Don't hide from the guilt of sin. See it first; then see that Christ has come to remove the problem of sin. He died in our place. He paid the wages of sin.

So the second part of the story is a rising. As Christ rose from the dead, so also we have a new life. We have a new life now as we live with the promise that Christ is with us. We have a life that will not be destroyed by old age, sickness, and death.

Life without Christ is a rising and fall. Life with Christ is a fall and rising. Christmas tells us that we can have the life with Christ. His name has been added to the cast of characters in your life, because He was born as a person like you. There will still be conflict and sadness in the story of your life, because you are still a sinner. But with Christ in the story of your life, you will have a victory over the problems of life.

You Don't Have a "Toy Savior"

The Word

At the end of eight days, when He was circumcised, He was called Jesus, the name given by the angel before He was conceived in the womb. Luke 2:21 (the Gospel for the Circumcision and the Name of Jesus)

The World

A toy iron (one that does not actually heat) and a real iron.

Do you know what this is? (Hold up toy iron.) It is an iron, right? If your grandmother had given you this for Christmas, you would have said to her, "Thank you for the iron." If you couldn't find it, you would say, "Where is my iron?"

But if this is an iron, then what is this? (Hold up real iron.) Obviously, these are not the same. Even though they do look a little alike, there is a big difference between them. The big difference is that one works and one doesn't. This is a real iron. It is to be used for ironing. This is a toy iron. It is for pretend ironing.

It is important for you to know that another gift you received for Christmas is real and not a toy. That gift is Jesus, who is God's gift of a Savior to you. He is not a toy Savior. He is the real Son of God, who became also a real human being to die for real sin.

Our text shows us how Jesus was our real Savior from the time He was a baby. When He was 8 days old, Mary and Joseph took Him to the temple to be circumcised. There was a Jewish law that said all boy babies had to be circumcised when they were 8 days old. Circumcision was a way of marking a person, by removing a small piece of skin, to show that he was a part of God's chosen people, the Jews. Jesus would not have had to be circumcised for Himself. He was already God's Son and needed no further mark to show that He belonged to God. But He came to obey the Law for us; therefore He started at the beginning and was circumcised. He continued to obey the Law for us in every way. Throughout His life He kept the Law perfectly and gives us credit for His obedience.

Because He obeyed the Law perfectly, He was named Jesus. Jesus means "Savior." The angel had told both Mary and Joseph that He should be named Jesus. Other Jewish boys were also named Jesus. Some of them may have fulfilled the meaning of the name, since there are many kinds of saviors. There are saviors who can save you from drowning or from some sicknesses. There are saviors who can protect you from fire and car wrecks. But Jesus is the Savior from sin. All other saviors only protect you from one problem, and life has more than one problem. But Jesus gets to the heart of the matter by removing the guilt that separates us from God. He is the Savior in a complete sense.

Don't treat Jesus like a toy savior. Don't use Him for pretend problems. Don't be excited about the gift for a while and then forget it. Jesus is a real Savior. He forgives your sins. He is needed every day of your life.

The Kind of Help That God Gives

The Word

Now when they had departed, behold, an angel of the Lord appeared to Joseph in a dream and said: "Rise, take the Child and His mother, and flee to Egypt, and remain there till I tell you; for Herod is about to search for the Child to destroy Him." And he rose and took the Child and His mother by night, and departed to Egypt, and remained there until the death of Herod. Matthew 2:13-15 (from the Gospel for the Sunday After New Year)

The World

A boy and a crutch.

I have asked Bill to help me today. Each of you boys and girls imagine that what happens to him is also happening to you. Have you ever had a broken bone, Bill? That can hurt. But it also has other problems. A broken bone can keep you from doing what you want to do. Let's suppose that your right leg is broken. That means that you can't walk on it. Pick up your right foot. See, it is hard enough to stand on one foot. You can't walk at all.

But look what I have for you. (Give him the crutch.) With this crutch and a little practice you could walk anywhere you wanted to go. If your leg were really broken, you would be glad to have that crutch. But if someone were to tell you to thank God for the crutch, you might wonder why God helped you by giving you the crutch. If He wanted to help, He could have given more help by preventing your leg from being broken in the first place.

We often wonder why God gives the kind of help He does. We are glad that He has sent cures for sickness, but

25

wouldn't it have been even better if He had destroyed sickness itself? We are thankful that He sent Jesus to be our Savior from sin. But why didn't He just destroy the devil and those who followed him in the first place?

Our text tells of another strange way that God helped someone. Soldiers were coming to kill the baby Jesus. God tells Joseph of their plans; so Joseph takes Jesus and Mary to Egypt to escape. God helped. But couldn't He have helped by stopping the soldiers so the Holy Family would not have had to make that long trip to Egypt?

In each of these cases we learn something important about the way God helps us. He has not destroyed evil. We can be glad for that. If God would have destroyed the devil and those who followed him, then God's answer to evil would have been destruction. But God is a creator, not a destroyer. If He would have destroyed evil, He would have had to destroy us too, because we have done evil.

Instead of destroying evil, God overcame it by sending Christ to pay the price of sin. Christ's resurrection from the dead destroys the power of evil over us but does not destroy us. Instead He saves us. God's answer to evil is not to destroy but to forgive.

In many other ways God is willing to accept the problems we have created. He stays with us and helps us even though we have not always followed His Word. He can still be God even if things don't always go His way. Our problems do not make Him leave us. Instead He offers help in the situations sin has caused.

Maybe we don't always understand why God helps us in the way He does. But we know that He helps, because we know that He cares. We know that there is no problem too big for Him. He is willing to live with us in all our difficulties and promises us a final victory.

Why Follow the Star?

The Word

Now when Jesus was born in Bethlehem of Judea in the days of Herod the king, behold, Wise Men from the East came to Jerusalem, saying: "Where is He who has been born King of the Jews? For we have seen His star in the East and have come to worship Him." Matthew 2:1-2 (from the Gospel for the Epiphany of Our Lord)

The World

Jar of peanut butter, two slices of bread, and a knife.

Suppose you arrive home after school and, as usual, are hungry. You look around and find a jar of peanut butter, then some bread; then to the drawer for a knife, and you're in business. Anybody can make a peanut butter sandwich. After you make it, you put the top back on the jar, put the jar away, and drop the knife into the sink — and there you are with your sandwich. But you forgot. You don't like peanut butter sandwiches. That would be silly, wouldn't it? Why go to all the trouble to make the sandwich when you will not eat it?

The same thing can be true of religion. Our religion puts us to a lot of bother. We have to get up and come to church, read the Bible, study Sunday school and confirmation lessons, do church work. Before you go through all that trouble you should know why you are doing it.

We can find a reason in our text. Some Wise Men from the East saw the star that announced the birth of Christ. They knew its meaning, and they followed it. That was a lot of trouble. They had to leave home, family, and job. They traveled a long distance. But it was worth it to them. They wanted to worship the newborn King. If they had wanted to make money, the trip would not have been worthwhile. If they had wanted to meet famous people and get honor for themselves, the trip would have been wasted effort. But they wanted to worship the Christ. They worshiped Him by showing their happiness about His birth. They worshiped Him by speaking of Him to others. They worshiped Him by giving Him gifts. Their trip was worthwhile. They were able to do what they wanted.

You and I also have something to follow. Instead of a star we have the life of Christ. We have heard about His birth. Now we will follow the events of His life. We will see His great miracles, hear His teachings, and learn more of His love for all people. There is a reason for studying the life of Christ. It is not just to learn some facts so someday you may win a prize on a quiz show. It is not just to learn some rules of what you should do and should not do. The reason is that we might see who Jesus really is and that, knowing Him, we might also worship Him.

Our worship of Christ is our response to who He is. When we see His miracles, we recognize Him as God; therefore we praise Him. When we hear His teachings, we receive the grace He has given us; therefore we thank Him and serve Him. When we know that He died for us and lives again, we know that He lives in us and uses our lives to continue His work. Just as you don't make a sandwich and then not eat it, so don't just see the things about Jesus without also worshiping Him. Worship Him with your words and your actions.

Do You Know Where to Look?

The Word

When they saw Him they were astonished; and His mother said to Him: "Son, why have You treated us so? Behold, Your father and I have been looking for You anxiously." And He said to them: "How is it that you sought Me? Did you not know that I must be in My Father's house?" Luke 2:48-49 (from the Gospel for the First Sunday After the Epiphany)

The World

A dictionary.

Most of you boys and girls have already learned how to use a dictionary. A dictionary has many purposes—to learn the meaning of a word, how to pronounce a word, how the word is correctly used in a sentence. Dictionaries are also supposed to be used to learn how to spell words. When you can't spell a word, often a teacher or parent will say: "Look it up in the dictionary."

But that presents a problem. To find a word in the dictionary, you have to know how it is spelled, or at least know the first few letters. Take the word *pneumonia,* for example. That's a difficult word to spell. It sounds like it should start with an *n.* From the sound, one would think it should be spelled *n-u-m-o-n-i-a.* But you can search that part of the dictionary, and you will not find it. Some of you know that to find *pneumonia* in the dictionary, you have to look under *p-n-e-u.* If you know that it starts with a *p-n,* you at least know where to look for the word.

In our text for today Mary and Joseph were looking for their young Son, Jesus. They spent several days searching for Him, looking in all the places where they thought a 12-year-old boy might be. They finally found Him in a place they had not expected Him to be. He was in the temple. Jesus seemed surprised that they had to search for Him at all. They should have known He would be in His Father's house. They had remembered that Jesus was a boy, but they had forgotten that He was also the Son of God. They didn't know where to look because they had forgotten who it was they were looking for.

We also have to know what we are looking for in our religion to know where to look. People often say that they have searched for spiritual understanding for years but have never found it. But when you ask them where they looked, you often find that they looked only into their own minds. We can't find God by looking to ourselves. Nor can we find God in a world that has rejected Him.

We can find God only because He has found us. He found us by sending Christ to become our Savior from sin. You find God in your baptism as you remember that in your baptism you put on Christ. You find God in the message of Scripture, which tells you of Christ's love and life for you. You find God in other Christians who are willing to speak of their own faith in Christ and to show their faith in the way they live.

Know what you are looking for. Then you can know where to look. Search for the peace that Christ has offered to all. Find it in the power of His Word.

It's Easy If You Know How

The Word

Jesus said to them, "Fill the jars with water." And they filled them up to the brim. He said to them, "Now draw some out, and take it to the steward of the feast." So they took it. When the steward of the feast tasted the water now become wine, and did not know where it came from (though the servants who had drawn the water knew), the steward of the feast called the bridegroom and said to him: "Every man serves the good wine first; and when men have drunk freely, then the poor wine; but you have kept the good wine until now." This, the first of His signs, Jesus did at Cana in Galilee, and manifested His glory; and His disciples believed in Him. John 2:7-11 (from the Gospel for the Second Sunday After the Epiphany)

The World

A large piece of paper on a clipboard, and a marker pencil.

Do any of you know how to add four 9s together to make 100? The answer must be exactly 100, no more and no less. It seems impossible, because if you just add the four 9s together like this, 9 plus 9 plus 9 plus 9, the answer is only 36. Yet as soon as you put two of them together to make 99 you cannot add another 9 without going way over 100. It seems impossible. Yet it can be done.

The solution is easy. You put down 99, which uses two 9s; then add 9/9 to it. Of course 9/9 equals 1; so 99 and 9/9 equals 100. See how easy it is? Just a few minutes ago it seemed impossible. Now it is simple. It is simple now, because you know how.

There is a problem in our text that also seems impossible. Jesus told some servants to fill six stone jars with water.

There was nothing in the jars except water; nothing was added except water. However, when the servants filled a pitcher from those same jars and took it to someone else who drank it, the water had changed to wine. The jars that were filled with water now contained wine.

That would be a difficult trick to do. If you saw a magician do it, you would know there is some explanation. Maybe he hid some wine concentrate, if there is such a thing, in the jars. There is *some* way to explain it.

Jesus was not a magician. But He *is* God. So the explanation is simple: Since Jesus is God, He has God's power, and God's power can do anything, even change water into wine. Jesus did this and many other miracles to show that He is God.

There are other things that are also impossible for us to understand. Why does God love me? How could Jesus' death pay for the sins of the whole world? How can we live forever? These things are impossible for us to understand. But that does not mean they are not true. We know these things, because Jesus has told us. Their truth depends on His truth, and He is God. Because we do not understand many things does not mean they are not true. It only means that God is far greater than we are. But He has not let His greatness separate Himself from us. He comes to us to share with us the blessings of His presence.

How Far Can You Trust Jesus?

The Word

A centurion came forward to Him, beseeching Him and saying, "Lord, my servant is lying paralyzed at home, in terrible distress." And He said to him: "I will come and heal him." But the centurion answered Him: "Lord, I am not worthy to have You come under my roof; but only say the word, and my servant will be healed." . . . When Jesus heard him, He marveled and said to those who followed Him: "Truly, I say to you, not even in Israel have I found such faith." . . . And to the centurion Jesus said: "Go; be it done for you as you have believed." And the servant was healed at that very moment. Matthew 8:5-8, 10, 13 (from the Gospel for the Third Sunday After the Epiphany)

The World

Fifty cents in coins and a billfold with $15.

Will each of you children pretend that you are lost downtown. You have no money with you. But then you see me. I am sure you are glad to see someone you know. You explain your problem and ask for help. Maybe all you need is a dime to phone home. I have a dime; so I can help you. Maybe there is no one home for you to call; so you need bus fare. Here is some more change, which should get you home. But there may be no bus going near your home. A taxi costs more money. Here is two dollars. But what if you have to go to another city, or to another part of the country, or overseas? The cost will get higher and higher, and soon I won't be able to help any longer. I have only $15 in my billfold, so I can't give you more than that. You can trust me to help only as far as I am able to help.

33

We can also trust Christ as far as He is able to give help. No one knows how far Christ can go in giving help, because no one has ever found a limit to His willingness and His ability to help. During His ministry on earth He showed how He could be trusted for help. He cured people who were sick. Many learned that He had power over sickness when He touched a sick person or spoke to one who was ill. Then in today's text we see how a centurion trusted Him even more. The centurion came to tell about his servant who was sick back home. This man knew that Jesus could heal the servant without touching him or speaking to him or even going near him. The centurion recognized that Jesus healed by the power of God and that such power could not be limited to one place. Jesus did as the man asked. The servant was made well.

By this miracle Jesus showed that His power was not limited to those who could actually see Him. Later, when He raised the dead back to life, He again expanded the power and love He was offering to people on this earth. With each miracle He removed the limits man had placed on His ability to help.

When we think of Jesus today, we are not to limit His love for us or His willingness to help us. The more we see of His power the more we can trust Him. Remember how He has loved you and died for you that you can be forgiven. Hear His promise that you will live with Him forever.

There is a limit to how much anybody else can help you. The person on earth who loves you most cannot give you more than he has. The best doctor cannot cure every sickness. All have limitations. But Christ has no limit. He has even gone through death for you that you might live with Him forever.

When Will You Ask for Help?

When He got into the boat, His disciples followed Him. And behold, there arose a great storm on the sea, so that the boat was being swamped by the waves; but He was asleep. And they went and woke Him, saying, "Save, Lord; we are perishing." And He said to them: "Why are you afraid, O men of little faith?" Then He rose and rebuked the winds and the sea; and there was a great calm. And the men marveled, saying, "What sort of man is this, that even winds and sea obey Him?" Matthew 8:23-27 (the Gospel for the Fourth Sunday After the Epiphany)

The World

A large replica of a stopwatch with movable second, minute, and hour hands.

Some of you may have seen a stopwatch. This is not a real stopwatch, but it will show you how a real one works. There will then be a special way to use this one. Other watches measure time by telling what time of day it is. A stopwatch doesn't tell the time of day. Instead it tells the time between two events. For example, a coach could start the watch by pushing this button at the beginning of a race. The second hand would go around once; then the minute hand would move one space. If the race were long enough for the minute hand to go around once, the hour hand would move one space. When the coach punched the button again, it would stop. Then he could see how many hours, minutes, and seconds the race had lasted.

I call this a spiritual stopwatch. See how it works. When you first learn that you have a problem, the clock starts moving. Seconds tick into minutes and minutes into hours.

35

The clock continues marking time until you ask God to help you with your problem.

The disciples in our text knew they had a problem when the skies became dark while they were out in a boat. But they did not bother Jesus, because He was asleep. When the winds started, they still did not ask for help. Only when they thought it was too late did they go to Him for help.

Do you do the same thing? How many minutes or hours do you delay in asking Him to help you? How long do you put off confessing your sins and asking for the forgiveness that you know God offers in Him? Jesus showed the disciples His power when He stilled the storm. They had seen His power in many other ways, but they still delayed asking Him for help until they were desperate.

Do you also delay? Perhaps the disciples could be excused, because Jesus was asleep and they did not want to wake Him. But God will always hear our prayers. Use the spiritual stopwatch as a reminder that you can ask God for help at all times. Do not delay in turning to Christ for help.

After you have asked God for help, you can use the spiritual stopwatch again. How long is it from the time you receive a blessing from God before you thank Him? Do hours and even days go by? Or do you sometimes fail to thank Him at all? The disciples may have delayed in asking Jesus for help, but they did not delay in praising Him for the help they received. They were amazed that He had power even over nature. They glorified God that He had sent this kind of help to people.

Use an imaginary spiritual stopwatch to remind you to ask God for help and to thank Him for the help He gives.

Saved for a Reason

The Word

Let both grow together until the harvest; and at harvesttime I will tell the reapers, Gather the weeds first and bind them in bundles to be burned, but gather the wheat into my barn. Matthew 13:30 (from the Gospel for the Fifth Sunday After the Epiphany)

The World

One hundred pennies in a sack.

The text is the last verse of a parable Jesus told about a farmer who planted good seed in his field. An enemy added bad seed. The farmer let both grow until the time of harvest, because if he pulled out the bad, he might also have destroyed the good. Jesus later explains this parable. He says it means that some people will receive the forgiving word of Christ. Others will follow the way of evil. Yet both will be allowed to live together.

Maybe we can understand this by looking at this sack of pennies. I am not a coin collector. Yet if I were told that one of the pennies in this sack was a rare coin, I would want to keep it. But there are a hundred pennies. And I am not able to tell which one is the rare coin. The only thing I could do is keep all the pennies until a coin collector examined them. Meanwhile, I would not dare spend a single penny. If I did, I might spend the rare penny. Even though I needed the money for something important, I could not spend any of these pennies.

In the same way we cannot wish for any person to be damned to hell, because we are not the ones who can judge such things. Even though we see evil, it is not our place to say that the person should be sent to hell. Even though someone has done something very bad, we have no right to damn him. When a man like King David committed the sins of murder and adultery, we might have thought that he was beyond hope. But later King David repented and was forgiven. We also might have wanted to damn the disciple Peter when he denied Jesus. But Jesus did not condemn him. Jesus forgave him. When we see evil in others, we are not to hand out God's punishment.

This does not mean that we should ignore evil. But we should treat the evil of others the way we treat our own. You are forgiven for your sin because Christ died for you. Christ also died for all other people. You are to respond to the other person's sin by offering the same forgiveness that you have.

In this way everyone is saved for a purpose. If you have received forgiveness from Christ, you are saved because you have a purpose in living. You can serve God by using the love He has given you. You can be like the wheat that was saved to bear fruit or the penny that was valuable.

But remember that God also has a reason for saving others. He loves them. He wants them to receive His love. He does not want to destroy them, because He not only loves them but by destroying them would destroy many who would later believe. He is the only one who can judge those who will never believe. He alone has the right to pronounce the final judgment of damnation to the one who rejects His grace in Christ.

Meanwhile we can be glad that we are already judged in Christ. Our judgment is based on Christ's holiness; we are declared free. We can share this freedom with others.

A Beautiful Sight—
Seen Through a Mess

The Word

After six days Jesus took with Him Peter and James and John his brother, and led them up a high mountain apart. And He was transfigured before them, and His face shone like the sun, and His garments became white as light. Matthew 17:1-2 (from the Gospel for the Last Sunday After the Epiphany)

The World

Two fine linen napkins from the same set, one dirty and crumpled, the other clean and neatly pressed.

Three disciples saw Jesus in a way they had never seen Him before. They had been with Jesus on the fishing boat. They were with Him when He ate, slept, traveled, and talked to people. They had seen Jesus perform miracles, but He still appeared to be an ordinary man. He may have had power that no other man had, but it didn't show when you looked at Him.

On this mountaintop they saw Jesus in a splendor they had never dreamed of. His face shone like the sun. Even His garments became radiantly white. A short time later Jesus again appeared to them as He always had—a regular man. They must have wondered which was the real Jesus.

Maybe we can understand this by looking at these two pieces of cloth. See this one. It is a beautiful napkin. You could put it on the table for the most fancy dinner party you ever had. It is clean and beautiful.

But look at this old rag. It is a mess. You might either throw it into the shoeshine box or into the garbage. But wait!

Take a closer look at it. This old rag is exactly the same cloth as this fine napkin. They come from the same set. One is ready for use. The other has been used. Which one is the real napkin? Both of them are. The one ready to be used will be messed up. The one that is messed up will be cleaned and ironed.

Which is the real Jesus? The Jesus whom the disciples knew in their everyday life was the real Jesus — the Jesus who was a man in the same way that they were men. But the Jesus whom they saw transfigured on the mountain was also the real Jesus — the Son of God, who became a man and yet remained God. He was the Savior, who did not always show His rightful glory as the Son of God but who nevertheless had it all the time.

Christ also comes to us in everyday, simple, sometimes even dull ways; yet in each coming there is a glorious, exciting, beyond-our-understanding event. In ordinary water and simple words written and spoken in our own language, He comes in baptism. Yet in that simple act He gives us the washing of a new birth and the gift of the Holy Spirit. In a book His words come printed in ordinary ink on the same paper as any other book; yet it brings a message of God's eternal love for you in Christ. In a Sunday school class where you wiggle and daydream like in any other class, something special occurs; for there you find that you are a child of God, created by Him, redeemed by Him, and loved by Him with a love that is far beyond our understanding.

Sometimes we get tired of the commonplace things in our religion. Sometimes we wonder if the great moments are really true or if we imagined them. But see them together. Only God can make such great news so simple that even we can understand it.

All This and Heaven Too

The Word

When evening came, the owner of the vineyard said to his steward: "Call the laborers and pay them their wages, beginning with the last up to the first." And when those hired about the eleventh hour came, each of them received a denarius. Now when the first came, they thought they would receive more; but each of them also received a denarius. Matthew 20:8-10 (from the Gospel for Septuagesima Sunday)

The World

Two brown paper bags: one containing a sandwich, apple, and cookies; the other containing an assortment of toys.

Jesus told a parable about a farmer who hired some men one morning to work in his field for a denarius a day. Later the farmer needed more help, so he found more men and promised to pay them what was right. Finally, about an hour before quitting time he found yet more workers, whom he sent to his field. At quitting time he called the men he had hired last and gave each a denarius — the price of a full day's work. The ones who had worked all day thought they would get more since they had worked more. But they also received a denarius. It seemed unfair, but the farmer reminded them that he had kept his agreement on what to pay them. They had no cause to complain.

Maybe we can understand this parable better by looking at these two sacks. Pretend that they belong to two Boy Scouts who want to earn their hiking badge. About 10 o'clock in the morning the first boy stops to rest and looks into the sack. The sight of the sandwiches, apple, and cookies assures him that he will have something to eat. At noon he arrives at his destination, sits down, and eats his lunch.

Meanwhile the second boy started his trip and also stopped to rest. He peeked into his sack and instead of food he saw a toy boat and some trucks. He had picked up the wrong sack! He had gone too far to turn back; yet he was getting hungrier and hungrier. He was beginning to wonder if he would make it home again. When he arrived at his destination, he saw a car. There his mother was waiting with his lunch. She had noticed that he had taken the wrong one, and she had driven out with it.

The point is that both boys had the same lunch to eat at the same time. But one knew he would have lunch, and the other did not. So also the laborers in the parable all received the same pay. The ones who worked all day had the comfort of knowing they would have wages to take home to the family. The others had worried all day because they thought they would have nothing for their families that evening.

This parable teaches us who have been Christians all our lives not to resent another person who becomes a Christian only a short time before he dies. Both the person who was a Christian all his life and served God faithfully and the one who becomes a Christian shortly before he dies go to the same heaven. Both are saved by the same grace that God gives through Christ.

This is not unfair to those of us who serve Christ all our lives. The life with Christ on earth is also a joy. We have known His love and have given it to others. We can be glad that someone else can share the joy of being with Christ in heaven even if he did not always share it with us on earth.

Directions Are for Following

The Word

A sower went out to sow his seed; and as he sowed, some fell along the path, and was trodden under foot, and the birds of the air devoured it. And some fell on the rock; and as it grew up, it withered away, because it had no moisture. And some fell among thorns; and the thorns grew with it and choked it. And some fell into good soil and grew, and yielded a hundredfold. Luke 8:5-8 (from the Gospel for Sexagesima Sunday)

The World

A package of presweetened Kool Aid, a pitcher of water, a long spoon, and a glass.

In His parable of the Sower and the Seed Jesus shows us that the Word of God must not only be used but that it must be used to change our lives. Perhaps we could show this in a modern story—the parable of the Kool Aid. All of you have heard the ads for presweetened Kool Aid, which say that all you need is Kool Aid and water for a delicious, refreshing drink. I have Kool Aid and I have water, but (pour water into glass and sip it) it still tastes like plain water.

But then that is because I haven't put them together. So I will add the Kool Aid to the water. (Drop the package, unopened, into the water.) Now I stir it. (Pour water into glass, and sip.) It still tastes like water.

Let's try again. (Retrieve package, open it, and dump contents into water. Stir.) Now it looks like we are getting somewhere. We have what looks like a delicious, refreshing drink. I won't do it, because I don't want to make a mess, but suppose, after I mixed the Kool Aid and water, I spilled

43

all of it. Then I still would not have that delicious, refreshing drink. Only when the Kool Aid and water are mixed, poured into a glass, and drunk is the promise of a delicious, refreshing drink fulfilled. You know, they're right. It is delicious and refreshing.

Now let's imagine that the package of Kool Aid is the Word of God and you are the pitcher of water. God promises that He will give you eternal life through His Word. The Word has two messages for you: You are a sinner, and God still loves you and has sent Christ to forgive you. As long as you do not come in contact with the Word, the message will mean nothing to you. That would be like having the Kool Aid package here and the pitcher there.

But it is possible to hear the Word of God and still not be changed—like when I put the entire package into the pitcher. That happens when you study God's law but don't see your own sins; or when you study the Gospel but don't understand that Christ died for you.

Or you can apply the Law and the Gospel and still be afraid to do anything about it—like the pitcher of Kool Aid being spilled—which I didn't do but you can imagine. That would be like knowing you are guilty but being afraid to say, "I am sorry"; or knowing that Christ died for you but being afraid to trust in Him.

But when the Kool Aid was made and drunk, it fulfilled its purpose. So also when the Word of God is applied to you and you believe it, it has achieved its purpose. When you see your sin and see that God has given an answer to sin in Christ, the promise of God's Word has been kept. You have eternal life.

Take a Long-Range View

The Word

Taking the twelve, He said to them: "Behold, we are going up to Jerusalem, and everything that is written of the Son of Man by the prophets will be accomplished. For He will be delivered to the Gentiles, and will be mocked and shamefully treated and spit upon; they will scourge Him and kill Him, and on the third day He will rise." Luke 18:31-33 (from the Gospel for Quinquagesima Sunday)

The World

A game (as shown at right) drawn on a large board, a marker with tape to hold it in place on vertical board, a coin, and 10 marbles.

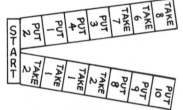

Some of you have played Put and Take. This is a different kind of Put and Take game. You have 5 marbles to begin with. You flip this coin. Heads means you move 2 spaces; tails gives you 1 move. You start here and can go either way you want. Okay, let's try it.

I flip the coin and have heads. If I go the top way, I will have to give 1 marble. If I go the bottom way, I will take 1 marble. Better go the bottom way. (Move marker and take 1 marble.) So I flip again. Heads again. I'll move 2 more this way and take 2 marbles. (Do so.) If I had been on the top, I would have had to put 3. Another flip. Tails. I move another space and have to put 8. That's all I have. If I had been on the top row, I would have taken 7. Let's try once more. Heads. I move here and have to put 10. But I don't have any marbles left. If I had been on the top I would have taken 8.

In this game it looked like a good idea to start out on the bottom row, but in the long run I would have been better off taking the top row. Even though I would have had to start out by giving marbles away, I would have ended up by getting them all back. Instead I was anxious to get a few at the beginning and then lost them all.

In our text Jesus shows that He is wiser. He says He is going to Jerusalem, where He knows He will be arrested, mistreated, and killed. It seems foolish for Him to go there if He knew what would happen. But He had a long-range view of life. He also knew that after His death He would rise again. He was willing to go through the difficulties, because they were necessary for Him to achieve His purpose of giving us eternal life. He had to die to win a victory over death.

From Jesus we can learn to take a long-range view of life. Sometimes we think only about today or next week. Say you have a choice between confirmation class and a ball game. The ball game is more fun. You have a choice between studying hard for a test and learning something, or cheating and getting the same grade. You can see which is easier. But that is the short-range view of life. Step by step you can go farther away from the final goal that you want. Take a long-range view of life.

The purpose of living is to be with God — to be with God not just in heaven but also now. Jesus did not promise an easy life for His followers. But He did say that those who suffer with Him will also be glorified with Him.

Don't trade away all of eternity for an easy day or week or year now. Christ has plans for you. He has given Himself so you could follow His plans. Follow Him!

Don't Be Tempted Alone

But He answered: "It is written, 'Man shall not live by bread alone, but by every word that proceeds from the mouth of God.'" . . . Jesus said to him: "Again it is written, 'You shall not tempt the Lord your God.'" . . . Then Jesus said to Him: "Begone, Satan! for it is written, 'You shall worship the Lord your God, and Him only shall you serve.'" Matthew 4:4, 7, 10 (from the Gospel for the First Sunday in Lent)

The World

Five or six sticks of various sizes, including small ones that can easily be broken, on up to thick ones that cannot be broken.

The story of Jesus' temptation by the devil is an exciting story for us, because for once the devil doesn't get his way. When we think of the times the devil tempts us, the story is less exciting and more embarrassing. But the story of Christ's temptation is more than a single event when Satan failed to get someone to follow him. It also helps us win victories today.

Let's look at it this way. A temptation is a form of a test. It is a trial to see whether or not a person has strength. Like this small stick. I can test its strength by trying to break it. See, I broke it easily. But this stick is larger. I can still break it. Maybe I can also break this one. But look at this stick. I can't possibly break it. It is too big.

Jesus is like the big stick. The devil couldn't break Him. We are like the little sticks. We fail the test. But just because we have failed does not mean that we should give up. It just tells us what company we should keep. If this little stick doesn't want to be broken, all it has to do is to be tested with the big stick. See, when the two are together, I can't break even the little one. When you don't want to be hurt by temptation, ask Christ to be with you in the time of temptation. Do this by being with fellow Christians and asking for their help. Do this by remembering your baptism and the help Christ has given you. Do this by reading His Word and finding comfort in the love He gives you.

Jesus shows us the power He used to fight temptation. In each case He answered the devil's temptation by quoting from the Bible. Remember that the devil also quoted Scripture, but Jesus used it to show that the power of God was on His side. We can also have the power of God on our side.

But Jesus did more than show us how to fight temptation. He actually fought the battle for us. He won, and He gives us His victory. When Jesus became a man, He became a member of our team. That is why He can be like the big stick and you like the small one. You belong together. He is willing to fight your battles for you. Be glad that He is on your side, and stay on His side.

A Lot of a Little—
Or a Little of a Lot

The Word

She said, "Yes, Lord, yet even the dogs eat the crumbs that fall from their master's table." Then Jesus answered her: "O woman, great is your faith! Be it done for you as you desire." And her daughter was healed instantly. Matthew 15:27-28 (from the Gospel for the Second Sunday in Lent)

The World

Two envelopes: one containing ten pennies, one containing four quarters.

If I were to give you the choice of these two envelopes, which would you take? I'll tell you this much: One envelope has ten coins in it, the other has four coins. Before you could make a correct choice you would have to know what coins are in each envelope. Let's look.

This one has ten coins. There are ten pennies which add up to a total value of ten cents. This envelope has only four coins, but they are quarters. The total value is one dollar. The first envelope had a large number, but they were of little value. The second had fewer coins, but they were of greater value. The choice was between a lot of a little or a little of a lot.

The woman in today's text had the same choice. She had a sick daughter. She loved her daughter and wanted to find help for her. Like most parents she would rather have been sick herself than see her daughter ill. The woman had probably gone to many people for help. She may have found some who wanted to help her. They could give her all the help that they knew how to give, but it still wasn't enough. No one could help her daughter.

Then she heard about Jesus. She asked Him for help. At first He ignored her. But she still asked for help. Then He told her it wasn't His job to help her, but she kept right on asking for help. Since she wasn't Jewish, He told her that it wasn't right to take food from the children's table and give it to dogs. She agreed and said she would be content if she could have just the crumbs. Think about what this woman was saying: Other people could offer all the help available, but it couldn't help her daughter; but from Jesus she wanted only a little of the great help she knew He had. Jesus gave her that help. He said she was a woman of great faith.

What about our faith? We have faith in many different ways — faith in family, friends, ourselves, our country. But faith can provide no more help than whatever we believe in is able to give. Often we find ourselves with a lot of faith in little things — like choosing the ten coins and getting ten cents.

But faith in Christ is different. No one has been able to measure the help that comes from Christ, because no one has reached the limit of His help. His help is too great to be measured in our ways of measuring things. Like the woman, we would be better off with a little help from Him than with all the help anyone else offers. To follow Christ may look like choosing the lesser of two ways of life. It takes humility and includes a cross. But it is like choosing the four coins — a lesser amount but of greater value.

No one else offers what Christ offers. He accepts you as you are. He makes you to be as He is.

Keep Your Life in Balance

The Word

He who is not with Me is against Me, and He who does not gather with Me scatters. Luke 11:23 (from the Gospel for the Third Sunday in Lent)

The World

A balancing scale (one can easily be made with Tinker Toys or an Erector set) and a number of blocks.

The text is a part of a discussion Jesus had with some religious leaders of His day. These men had accused Him of using the power of Satan to do great works. Jesus had pointed out that His works accomplished good things. Since Satan does not do good things, Jesus' power obviously came not from the devil but from God. But then He asked the men to think about their own action by saying, "He who is not with Me is against Me, and He who does not gather with Me scatters."

So that we can also apply Jesus' words to ourselves, let us look at this balancing scale. See, it is balancing now. When equal weights are added to each side (put two blocks, same size, on either side), it still balances. This side (your left) will represent God's side. This side (your right) will be the side of evil. Actually, good and evil do not balance. By His resurrection from the dead Christ has won the victory over Satan and the power of evil. The side of God has already won. But to help us understand our own involvement in the struggle and to see the need for Christ, we will start off with the scale in balance.

This block (the one on the left) represents the good you

are supposed to do. When you follow the commandments by not doing the things that are forbidden — not hating, not stealing, not using God's name in vain, and the like — you are putting your action on this side of the scale. When you do what you should — honoring your parents, loving others, telling others about Christ, and the like — you are putting your action on this side. However, when you do the opposite, when you do the things that have been forbidden and fail to do those things that are commanded, your action is on this side of the scale. (Move block from left side to right.) See what that does to the scale. It throws it out of balance in favor of evil.

You knew that when you did evil you worked on Satan's side. But Jesus goes one step further when He tells you: "He who is not with Me is against Me, and He who does not gather with Me scatters." Let's put this block back on the other side so the scale is balanced again. Many times in life we feel we can't do what God requires; but we don't want to do what is evil. Somehow we want to be neutral — doing neither good nor evil. When that happens, you are not doing good, so the block comes off this side. Now, even though you don't put the block on the side of evil, evil still wins out. By not doing what is good, you are automatically doing evil. There is no neutral position. You are either for Christ or against Him. You cannot hide from sin by doing nothing.

This shows us all the more why we need Christ so much. There is no way we can avoid all that is wrong. There is no way we can do all that is right. But Christ has come on this (left) side of the scale. He has placed His goodness on the line with us. (Put big block on left side.) The side of good wins, because He is on that side. He asks you to be on that side with Him.

Do You Know How to Use a Gift?

The Word

When they had eaten their fill, He told His disciples, "Gather up the fragments left over, that nothing may be lost." So they gathered them up and filled twelve baskets with fragments from the five barley loaves, left by those who had eaten. When the people saw the sign which He had done, they said, "This is indeed the prophet who is to come into the world." Perceiving then that they were about to come and take Him by force to make Him king, Jesus withdrew again to the hills by Himself. John 6:12-15 (from the Gospel for the Fourth Sunday in Lent)

The World

A camera wrapped as a birthday gift, several books, and a bookend.

Pretend it is your birthday and this is a gift from your grandmother. I know you'd be anxious to open it, so I'll unwrap the package. Look, a camera! Imagine how your grandmother would feel if you said: "Thank you for the camera. I know just how I'm going to use it. See, I have only one bookend for my books. I'm going to use the camera for the other bookend. See how it holds up the books. Thank you, that's exactly what I needed."

It would be a shame to use such a nice camera as a bookend. That's not the way to use a gift. The people in our text also used a gift in a wrong way. Remember the story? About 5,000 people were following Jesus to hear Him. They hadn't had anything to eat. The only food available belonged to a boy who had five loaves of bread and two fish. Jesus used the small amount of food to feed all 5,000 people. After they had eaten all they could, the disciples gathered up 12 baskets of leftover food.

That was a great miracle. The people were so impressed by it that they tried to make Jesus their king. But all they wanted from Him was food to eat. None of them stopped to wonder how Jesus could perform such a miracle. They just figured that if He could do it once He could do it again. They would never have to work again. They were about as foolish as a child using a camera as a bookend. They had an opportunity to be near the Son of God. He was offering them more than bread, which would only satisfy for one day. He wanted to give them Himself, the Bread that would give life to the world. But all they wanted was bread for the stomach. When He refused to be their king, many left Him.

People today also often get angry at Christ because He won't do what they want. A student prays for straight A's and ends up with B's and C's; so he is disappointed in God. A boy playing ball prays to make a home run but strikes out. Why, God? Why? A girl asks for a new dress and gets a hand-me-down from her fat cousin. Why, God?

Have you been disappointed in God? Maybe you misunderstand His gifts. Maybe you are using a camera as a bookend. He has given you His love in Christ. He has promised that He will be with you forever. He will never leave you. He does care about report cards and ball games and new dresses. Remember He also cared about feeding the 5,000 people. But God sees life as more than having food for one day, or one home run, or one wish come true. He wants to make you happy for more than a day or a week. He wants you with Him forever. That's why He gave you Christ. Always see the Savior as the greatest gift; then you can enjoy whatever else you may happen to have.

What You Don't Know Can Hurt You

The Word

He who is of God hears the words of God; the reason why you do not hear them is that you are not of God. John 8:47 (from the Gospel for the Fifth Sunday in Lent)

The World

A 10-year-old child, a clipboard, and a marker pencil (a blindfold if it is not convenient to have the child leave the room).

I have asked Lynn to help me today. First of all, Lynn, you may help by stepping outside for a few minutes (or putting on the blindfold). Now while Lynn can't see, I am going to write something on this piece of paper so all of you can see it. (Write: GOD LOVES YOU.) Can you all see the words? Don't say them out loud. Those of you who are too small to read may ask your mother or someone to tell you what the words say. Now I will fold the paper so no one can see the words. But you remember what it said.

Lynn, you may come back in now. Do you know what it says on this piece of paper? Everyone else in the room knows but you. The reason everyone else knows is that they saw me write the words. You didn't, of course, because you were out of the room. Our text describes why some people know things and others don't. In this case it could say: "Those who were in the room know the words on the paper; the reason you do not know the words is because you were not in the room." Since you are back in the room now, I'll give you the paper and you may return to your seat.

Remember why you knew what the paper said and why

Lynn didn't know as you hear the text again: "He who is of God hears the words of God; the reason why you do not hear them is that you are not of God." Do you know God's Word? Do you know the Commandments, which tell you what to do and what not to do? Do you know the Law, which says that all people are guilty before God? Do you know that Christ has kept the Law for you and paid the price of your sin by dying on the cross for you? If you know these things, then you are of God. That means God has worked through His Word to make you His own. The Holy Spirit uses the Word of God to make you see your sin and then to see your Savior.

But it also says that if you do not hear the Word of God, you are not of God. Of course, you are all in church; so you hear the Word of God here. But do you pay attention and apply it to yourself? You should also hear the Word of God more than once a week. You can read the Bible at home. You can have family devotions. You can attend Sunday school. He who is of God hears the words of God.

As you grow older you will also have to decide for yourself whether or not you will attend church and Sunday school. Remember how important it is that you continue to hear the Word of God. Also if you ever feel that God has left you, ask yourself if you have left His Word. Then you may see that God never leaves us. But sometimes people do leave God.

But if you remain with His Word, you will remain in the love that Christ has given you.

In the Yellow Pages — Under "Savior"

The Word

This took place to fulfill what was spoken by the prophet, saying, "Tell the daughter of Zion, Behold, your King is coming to you, humble, and mounted on an ass, and on a colt, the foal of an ass." Matthew 21:4-5 (from the Gospel for Palm Sunday)

The World

A phone book that includes the Yellow Pages.

Do you already know how to use the Yellow Pages in the phone book? They can help you in an emergency or even just to get something done quicker. Suppose you need a doctor, for example. You could look under "Physicians" and find a list of all the doctors in town. Or if you want to check the prices of baseball bats, you look under "Sports Equipment." The Yellow Pages have many uses.

Wouldn't it be nice if you could find Jesus by looking in the Yellow Pages? You'd look under "Savior," and there He would be listed: "Jesus Christ, the Savior of the World." Of course, you know that He is not listed in the Yellow Pages. But remember that the people of Jerusalem did look Him up in a book, and that's how they were able to find Him.

They didn't look in a phone book, but they looked in the writings of the prophets — the prophets Isaiah and Zechariah. These prophets, and others, had written many years before that a Messiah would come who would save the people from their sin. The words of our text are part of their prophecies: "Tell the daughter of Zion" — that means the people of the city of Jerusalem — "Behold, your King is coming to you, humble, and mounted on an ass, and on a colt, the foal of an ass."

That is a strange prophecy. Kings are not humble, as a rule. They do not ride on donkeys. Kings are proud and have grand chariots. But this is about a special king — one who was born of a virgin, one who was to be offered as a sacrifice for the sin of the world. The people of Jerusalem recognized Him as He entered their city. They rejoiced that the Savior had come. They put palm branches and their own clothing on the street to make a carpet for His donkey. It was a great day for them. They had looked under "Prophecy" and had found a Savior.

Today is a great day for us too. Though we can't find "Savior" listed in the Yellow Pages, we do have a place to look for Him. You can look in the New Testament under "Matthew," "Mark," "Luke," or "John" and find how He lived, how He died, and how He lives again. You can look under "Acts" and see how His work is continued by the power of the Holy Spirit in the lives of people long after He ascended into heaven. You can look under "Romans" or "Ephesians" or "1 John" to see how His life changes your life today.

If you were in need of a doctor, it would be a relief to find one through the Yellow Pages. You are in need of a Savior. What a joy it is to have found where He is listed. As He was welcomed into Jerusalem, so He can be welcomed into our lives, our homes, our community. We have a Savior. Let's be glad about it!

It Is Finished

The Word

When Jesus had received the vinegar, He said, "It is finished"; and He bowed His head and gave up His spirit. John 19:30 (from the Gospel for Good Friday)

The World

A bowl of pudding, a can of whipped cream, nutmeats.

One of the last things Jesus said from the cross before His death was, "It is finished." These words could have at least two meanings. Let's try to understand them by using the same words in a different situation.

Here is a bowl of pudding. Someone else has already partly made it, but it is not quite done yet. I am going to add some whipped cream. Then I put some nuts on top. Now I can say, "It is finished." That means that the pudding is completed. All the work is done, and the pudding is ready to be eaten. That is one meaning of "It is finished."

I won't eat in front of you, since that wouldn't be polite. But suppose I ate the pudding. After I finished the last spoonful, I could say, "It is finished." That would mean that the pudding was gone. It was all eaten. That is another meaning of "It is finished."

Which of these two thoughts did Jesus mean when He said, "It is finished"? Those who heard Him probably thought that He meant the last one. It is finished. His life was over. His teachings had ended. His friendships were gone. His miracles had ceased. Like the pudding, He appeared to be "all gone." It could have looked that way to those who were there on the first Good Friday.

But it has never looked that way on a Good Friday since then. We know what happened 3 days later. He knew that His life was not finished. His friendships had not ended. His teaching was not stopped. His miracles had not ceased.

When Jesus said, "It is finished," He was speaking of a job that He had completed. It was a job that started in the Garden of Eden many centuries before, when the first man and first woman committed the first sin. From that time on, man had one big job to do. He had to get back to God. He had to rid himself of his own guilt. Men worked in many ways to complete such a task. But they couldn't do it.

Then Jesus came, as God had promised He would. By becoming a man He took the burden of our sin upon His shoulders. The burden crushed Him down into death. But He took the burden from all others. As He died, He felt the burden upon Himself, but He also felt the burden being removed from all others. And He said, "It is finished." Salvation is complete. Man and God are reunited in Jesus Christ.

Some people still want to work on the job of their own salvation. They still try to work their own way back to God. They do it by leaving Jesus out or by using Him only as a teacher who tells us how to save ourselves. But He is more than a teacher. He is the Savior. He accepted the job of saving man. And He says the job is finished!

After the End Comes the Beginning

The Word

He said to them: "Do not be amazed; you seek Jesus of Nazareth, who was crucified. He has risen, He is not here. . . . But go, tell His disciples and Peter that He is going before you to Galilee; there you will see Him, as He told you." Mark 16:6-7 (from the Easter Gospel)

The World

Two identical pictures (Easter church bulletins will do), black crayon, match, metal tray.

The message of the angel from the tomb on the first Easter is amazing in many ways. It's amazing enough just to have an angel talk to us. But listen to what he had to say. He admitted that Jesus had been crucified. He did not ignore the fact that there had been death. But the angel refused to regard death as the end. Speaking of the Jesus who had been crucified, the angel said: "He is going before you to Galilee; there you will see Him."

To help us understand the angel's words, we will use this picture to represent human life—the life we all share together. It is a beautiful picture. God gave us a beautiful life; it was even perfect. Then we messed the picture up. (Mark across the picture with the crayon. Crumple it.) The beautiful life God had given us was ruined. Our sin destroyed God's beauty. By our rebellion against His authority we refused the good that He had given us.

That's when Jesus came into the picture. He became human—a part of this messed-up life. He died in our place. Death means that life is destroyed. (Burn the crumpled picture over the tray.) Death destroyed the sin and trouble that man had added to life, but, you see, it also destroyed life itself.

But then comes the message of Easter. (Hold up the other picture.) Life has not been destroyed. It has been restored. The One who died lives again. Instead of death being the end, it became the way for a new beginning. Death took sin to the grave. Life came back without the sin. You know, of course, that this picture is not the same one that was burned. It is another picture that looks the same. But it was the same Christ who both died and lived again. And in that order! He has shown that sin can be destroyed without destroying life itself. He has taken the threat of punishment from us by removing our punishment. He has shown us that we need no longer fear the grave. It will not be the end. It will be the opportunity to have a new beginning.

This new beginning can also be a part of our daily lives. Yesterday's guilt, the sorrows of the past, the failures that make us afraid to try again do not have to destroy us. They are ended. After the end comes a new beginning. We have that new start in Christ. He has given us His new life. Let us live it with Him!

Seeing Is Not Believing

The Word

Then He said to Thomas: "Put your finger here, and see My hands; and put out your hand, and place it in My side; do not be faithless, but believing." Thomas answered Him: "My Lord and my God!" Jesus said to him: "Have you believed because you have seen Me? Blessed are those who have not seen and yet believe." John 20:27-29 (from the Gospel for the First Sunday After Easter)

The World

A sack of seven marbles.

This sack has some marbles in it. (Shake sack.) Your job this morning is to find out how many marbles are in the sack. There are three ways you could find out. First, you could guess. Of course, you would not know for sure that your guess was correct; but if you were satisfied with it, you could go on and think that you were right. Next, I could tell you how many marbles there are in the sack. Seven is the correct answer. You could believe me. Or you could demand proof and count them. (Dump marbles into hand.) You count them as I drop them back into the sack. One, two, three, four, five, six, seven.

Now let's apply these three ways of knowing something to the resurrection of Christ. The three ways are: guessing, knowing, and believing. To rely on guesswork is to show that you don't care. To just guess at something without bothering to find the truth is to say that it is unimportant. We can have no guesswork about the resurrection of Christ.

The other two ways are the subject of our text. Ten of

the disciples had seen the risen Savior. They knew He had risen, just like you know there are seven marbles in that sack. You counted the marbles. They saw a man who had been dead but was alive again. Thomas was not with them, but they told him about the resurrection. He had not seen, but he had been told—just as I told you how many marbles were in the sack. He could have believed. But he didn't. He demanded the same proof that the others had had.

Jesus came to him and gave him the proof. When Thomas saw Him, he said: "My Lord and my God!" Then he believed. But Jesus said: "Have you believed because you have seen Me? Blessed are those who have not seen and yet believe." We might think that our faith is weaker than Thomas'. We believe something we have not seen, but he believed something he had seen. But Jesus says that it is the other way around. Our faith is stronger, because we can believe what we have not seen.

If we could believe only what we see, we could accept neither the past nor the future. We can see only the present. But faith is seeing with the heart. It is knowing that things have happened and things will happen. Faith recognizes that there are things that cannot be seen but yet are true. The demand to believe only what you see always puts doubt on tomorrow, because you cannot see tomorrow until it comes. But faith says that tomorrow presents no problems, because Christ still lives with us.

Faith is not based on guesswork. Faith is based on the fact of Christ's death and resurrection for you. Faith accepts what God has done in Christ as a truth that has not changed and will not change. "Blessed are those who have not seen and yet believe."

The Shepherd Who Leads

The Word

I am the Good Shepherd. The Good Shepherd lays down His life for the sheep. . . . And I have other sheep, that are not of this fold; I must bring them also, and they will heed My voice. So there shall be one flock, one Shepherd. John 10:11, 16 (from the Gospel for the Second Sunday After Easter)

The World

A child, two theater tickets.

In our text Jesus tells us that He is the Good Shepherd and we are His sheep. Notice: He did not say that He is the Shepherd and we are the good sheep, but He is the Good Shepherd and we are the sheep. There is a big difference between the two. If we were the good sheep, it would mean that we are good followers. If He is the Good Shepherd, it means that He is a good leader.

To show the difference between good followers and good leaders, I will ask Randy to come and help me. Randy, I want you to follow me. (Walk across the room.) See, Randy is a good follower. Now let's see how far Randy could follow me. If I walked out and got in my car, could you follow me? Sure you could. If I drove downtown, you would be following in the back seat. If I got out of the car and walked around the block, you could follow. You could follow me into a department store, up the elevator, down the stairs, and wherever I went. All this would show that you are a good follower.

But suppose I walked to a theater. Remember, you are

still following me, Randy. I give the man at the door one ticket (show ticket), and I go inside. Are you still following me? The man at the door would stop you. You are no longer a good follower.

Suppose that instead of giving the man one ticket I gave him two. (Show other ticket.) Then you could still follow me. You could follow not because you are a good follower but because I am a good leader. I bought the ticket for you so you could follow.

Jesus is the Good Shepherd, because He laid down His life for the sheep. As our Shepherd He wants to lead us to heaven. But He cannot depend on our ability to follow Him. He is holy, the Son of God. We are sinners, which puts us on a different road. We cannot follow Him to heaven, because our sin stops us. But He buys the ticket. He gives His holiness for us to use. We are going to heaven not because we are good sheep but because He is the Good Shepherd.

Jesus tells us that He wants to be the Good Shepherd for all people. He did not have just two tickets, like I did when Randy followed me. He gave His life for all people. He says that He has many other sheep, which are not yet following Him, but He wants them to join Him. When you show others why you follow Jesus, you are encouraging them also to follow Him. When you let others know what a Good Shepherd you have, let them also know that He is *their* Good Shepherd. Then we can all follow Him together.

Sorrow That Brings Joy

The Word

Truly, truly, I say to you, you will weep and lament, but the world will rejoice; you will be sorrowful, but your sorrow will turn into joy. John 16:20 (from the Gospel for the Third Sunday After Easter)

The World

A bat and ball.

Can you imagine the good feeling inside a baseball player when he steps up to the plate, leans back, and knocks the ball clear across the fence? I won't try to do it here, because I probably couldn't, and if I could, we'd have a broken window. Some of you may know the joy of hitting a home run, because you've done it. All of us can imagine it. It's great whether it's in a sandlot game for the kids in the neighborhood or in the world series of the major leagues.

But do you think any baseball player started out hitting home runs? You can also imagine the disappointment of going to bat and missing the first ball (swing and miss), the second (swing and miss), and the third (swing and miss). Three strikes and you're out, at the old ball game. And that gives the opposite feeling of a home run.

Yet if any ball player wants the joy of a home run, he has to be willing to have the sorrow of the strikeout. The same is true in many other areas of life. Jesus speaks of sorrow before joy in our text. He has been telling His disciples that He must suffer and die. They react against such an idea. They are afraid of the sorrow. But He tells them that the sorrow is not the purpose of His dying. He is willing to die to give them a joy far beyond any joy they have ever known or expected. By His death He promises to give them a victory over death. The joy of His resurrection will wipe out all the sorrow of His death.

Jesus spoke these words before His death to give the disciples strength to endure the sorrow they would feel when He died. He also speaks to us in our sorrows. Don't be afraid to live life; don't be afraid to love people, though there may be sorrow involved. If you avoid the sorrow, you will also avoid the joy of sharing life with others. Don't be afraid to follow Christ even when there is a cross. Without the cross there is no crown. Without sharing in Christ's sorrow we cannot understand His joy.

He does not say that all sorrow will automatically turn to joy. But the sorrow that is endured with Him will turn to joy. When you feel the sorrow of guilt and shame, include Christ in the sorrow. That is why He went to the cross — to share that sin and shame with you. Then you can share the joy of His resurrection — a victory over all guilt and shame. When you feel the sorrow of loneliness and fear, include Him in that sorrow. He removes the loneliness, for He is with you. He removes the fear, for your life is in His hands. When He is for you, who can be against you?

Help That Stays — By Going Away

The Word

Nevertheless I tell you the truth: it is to your advantage that I go away, for if I do not go away, the Counselor will not come to you; but if I go, I will send Him to you. John 16:7 (from the Gospel for the Fourth Sunday After Easter)

The World

A tray with five clear water glasses, each about two thirds full of water; and a clear pitcher, filled with water that has been heavily colored with food coloring or ink.

On the night before His death Jesus explained to His disciples not only that He would die and rise again, but also that He would no longer be with them in the way they were used to having Him. He even said that it would be to their advantage that He would leave, because then the Counselor, who is the Holy Spirit, would come to them. What Jesus said is important to us, because we have never been with Him as the disciples were. We sometimes think that they had the advantage over us, because they saw and touched Him. But Jesus says that it is to our advantage that we have the Holy Spirit's presence instead of Jesus' physical presence.

This can be illustrated by looking at this pitcher and these glasses. They are a set that belong together. The water in the pitcher will represent Christ. It is colored so you can see His presence. The water in the glasses represents His disciples. The disciples are with Jesus the way they were before His death. We see their symbols all on the same tray. But Jesus left them. (Remove the pitcher.) For a while the disciples were alone. Even though Jesus did come back from the dead, He never returned to live with them as He did before His death. Then, 40 days after His resurrection, He ascended into heaven. Yet Jesus had said: "Lo, I am with you always, even unto the end of the world."

Ten days later it happened. On Pentecost the Holy Spirit came as Jesus said He would. The Holy Spirit brought the presence of Christ to each disciple. (Pour from pitcher into each glass.) Now Jesus was not just *with* the disciples as He had been before. He was *in* each of them. The disciples did not have to stay together in one place to be with Jesus. Each could go a different way; yet Jesus would be with each of them.

By the power of the Holy Spirit the presence of Christ was no longer a place in geography, a spot on a map. No longer was His presence a matter of time — "I was with Jesus last week," or "I'll see Jesus next Thursday at 2 p. m." Jesus became present in all time and in all places. Jesus is everywhere people hear His Word and believe in Him.

We are like these disciples. (Hold up a glass.) The Holy Spirit has brought Christ into our lives. It is to our advantage that we don't have to go to Jerusalem to see Jesus. He is here. It is to our advantage that we know He can be with us here and also with our friends and family far from here. He is both here and there.

The Holy Spirit has come. Christ has sent Him to continue in us all things that Christ has done for us. He will never leave us.

Pray in His Name

The Word

Truly, truly, I say to you, if you ask anything of the Father, He will give it to you in My name. Hitherto you have asked nothing in My name; ask, and you will receive, that your joy may be full. John 16:23-24 (from the Gospel for the Fifth Sunday After Easter)

The World

Two library cards, one a child's and one an adult's (assuming that they are different colors; if not, make cards that are obviously different), and a stack of children's books.

Jesus says that we are to pray in His name. As Christians we always pray in the name of Christ. But we should not use His name as though it were a magic password to get our prayers heard. There is a good reason why we must always pray in His name. Maybe you can see this reason by pretending to go to the library with me.

I hope you all have been to the library and have a card like this one (child's card). As you go through the shelves you find several books that you want to take home. (Show books.) You take the books and the card to the librarian. But as she looks at your card, she frowns and checks your card number against a list on her desk.

"I'm sorry," she says, "but you can't check out any more books. The last time you checked out books, you returned them late, one had a page missing, and several had jelly smeared all over them." You tell her that you are sorry and that you'll do better the next time. But she still says that you can't have the books.

Just then your mother comes in to get you. The librarian

explains why you can't have the books. Your mother agrees that the librarian is right; however, your mother also believes that you will try to do better the next time. So she takes her library card (adult card) and gives it to the librarian. You still get your books, but you get them in your mother's name. She is accepting the responsibility for you. If you mess up the books, it will be on her card.

In the same way you have ruined your right to ask God for anything. You have not done what He has commanded. You have not served Him and loved Him as you should. You have not loved other people as He told you to. None of us have. I know you haven't, and I haven't either. But God still loves us. Christ has come to be our Savior. He has accepted the responsibility for our sin. Now He says that we can pray to God. We can pray, but not because we deserve it; we can't ask on our own card. But we can pray in *His* name; we *can* ask on *His* card.

Often we are afraid to ask God for help because we know we don't deserve it. But it would be just as bad to ask Him if we thought we did deserve it. Yet we can have His help, because He wants to give it. Christ has earned our right to pray to God. That is why we always pray "in the name of Christ" or "for Jesus' sake." When we ask in His name, we have the right to pray.

Who Makes the Rules?

The Word

But when the Counselor comes, whom I shall send to you from the Father, even the Spirit of truth, who proceeds from the Father, He will bear witness to Me; and you also are witnesses, because you have been with Me from the beginning. John 15:26-27 (from the Gospel for the Sunday After the Ascension)

The World

A child's game (the game "Blockhead" is used in this talk; however, any child's game that has rules for playing may be used).

This is a game called "Blockhead." Let's pretend that it belongs to your brother but he is letting you play with it. The idea is to see how many blocks you can stack up before they fall over. You start the game by putting these two small blocks down and then using this long one to make a bridge. Your brother comes along and says that you can't do that. He says you have to put the long one down first and then place the two on it. To settle the disagreement you read the rules on the box. It says that only one block may touch the table and only one block may touch the first block. From then on any number of blocks may be put on another block.

But the rules didn't settle the disagreement. You say that if you are playing you should get to play the way you want to. Your brother says that if you are playing with his game you should play his way. Your mother says you should play by the rules that came with the game.

It is hard to know what to do when you have conflicting rules. Sometimes we get the idea that we have conflicting rules in the Bible. We talk about God the Father and the

73

rules He gave us in the Old Testament. Then we study about His son, Jesus Christ, who came and gave us more than rules by His death and resurrection for us. That is another way of life. Then we have the Holy Spirit, who now continues the work of God in us. We are to rely on the Holy Spirit to guide us. Then we wonder: Is there a conflict in the way of life we receive through the Father, the Son, and the Holy Spirit?

Jesus says there is no conflict. Often during His ministry He emphasized that He did not come to teach a new doctrine but to fulfill all that God the Father had given Him to do. He says that the Holy Spirit proceeds from the Father and that He also brings the same truths to the hearts of men.

Jesus calls the disciples as witnesses that there is no conflict among the Persons of the Trinity. The disciples had grown up as Jews. They followed the Old Testament and did not regard themselves as converts when they found Christ as their Savior. Their religion had taught them to look for a Messiah. Now they found Him. After Pentecost the disciples found no conflict between what the Holy Spirit led them to do and what Christ had taught them. All their lives they looked for the reunion between God and man that the Father had promised. They found it in Christ. They lived it by the power of the Holy Spirit.

We cannot ignore the Old Testament on the excuse that the New Testament replaces it. We need both for the total message of God. We cannot ignore the New Testament on the basis that it is almost 2,000 years old and out of date. The Holy Spirit still brings us the same message of Christ's sacrifice for our sin. Through it we receive the very up-to-date message that today there is forgiveness. Today there is salvation — from God.

How Well Can You Remember?

The Word

These things I have spoken to you while I am still with you. But the Counselor, the Holy Spirit, whom the Father will send in My name, He will teach you all things and bring to your remembrance all that I have said to you. John 14:25-26 (from the Gospel for the Feast of Pentecost)

The World

Ten large pieces of paper on which the following words are printed: SPIRIT, PENTECOST, FLAMES, BAPTIZE, GRACE, CROSS, COUNSELOR, WATER, SAVIOR, FAITH; a wastebasket.

There is a word written on each of these 10 pieces of paper. Look at the words one at a time. (Show the words in the above order.) Now that you have seen the 10 words in order, I am going to tear up the paper and throw it away. (Shred the paper and throw it into the wastebasket.)

Now I want you to repeat back to me those 10 words in the same order. Can you do it? You probably feel something like Jesus' disciples did on the night before His death. He told them that He was going to leave them. They were not prepared for that. They had assumed that He would always be with them. Even though He had taught them many things, they could easily forget what He said or get the message mixed up, as they frequently did. He had explained some of His parables, but each of the disciples might remember the explanation in a different way. Jesus had not written anything down for them to restudy. Perhaps none of them had taken notes on His teachings.

You can see why the disciples were upset. They felt that the future of all His great teachings would depend on them.

The salvation of the world would depend on how well they remembered what Jesus had said and done. That was a big load for them. Just as you can't be sure that you can remember those 10 words in the same order — you probably couldn't even pronounce some of them — the disciples could not be sure that they could repeat all of Jesus' teachings.

But Jesus told them not to worry. He said: "These things I have spoken to you while I am still with you. But the Counselor, the Holy Spirit, whom the Father will send in My name, He will teach you all things and bring to your remembrance all that I have said to you."

The future of Christ's teachings did not depend on the disciples' memories. It depended on the power of the Holy Spirit. Your salvation today does not depend on how well the disciples remembered and repeated the words and actions of Jesus; it depends on the Christ who earned eternal life for you. Your knowledge of that salvation depends on the Holy Spirit, who brought it to the mind of the disciples as they recorded it for us in the pages of the New Testament. Your faith in that salvation is the result of the Holy Spirit's work in your heart.

On Pentecost Jesus' promise was fulfilled. The Holy Spirit came to the disciples and filled them with the power of Christ's message for the world. They spoke it boldly, and it is still heard today. If it were really important, we could repeat the 10 words in their proper order, because I have them written down. That is not important. But it is important that we can recheck the life of Christ. We can restudy what happened, and because the Holy Spirit guided the men who wrote the Bible, we can be sure that we have the true story of the events that took place in a far-off country 1,900 years ago.

A New Creation from an Old One

The Word

Jesus answered him: "Truly, truly I say to you, unless one is born anew, he cannot see the kingdom of God." Nicodemus said to Him: "How can a man be born when he is old? Can he enter a second time into his mother's womb and be born?" Jesus answered: "Truly, truly, I say to you, unless one is born of water and the Spirit, he cannot enter the kingdom of God." John 3:3-5 (from the Gospel for Trinity Sunday)

The World

An empty half-gallon milk carton, a sharp knife.

Nicodemus could not understand what Jesus meant when He said, "You must be born anew." It is difficult for us to understand too. It seems impossible for a person to be born a second time. Obviously, Jesus doesn't mean for a person to be born again physically. That would be only a repeat of our first birth with no improvement. He is talking about a new birth that is a different birth. Maybe an illustration will help.

This milk carton has already served its purpose. It was filled with milk and sold, and the milk was used. You can't return a carton, like a bottle, to be used again. The carton is to be thrown away, unless it can be saved by using it for another purpose. By cutting out one side of the carton (do so with the knife) and putting it on its side, the carton can be used as a flowerpot. With some dirt in it, it will serve a new purpose. It will not be thrown away.

In the same way each of us was born for a purpose. However, that purpose was not the one for which God had originally created man. By our birth our purpose is to serve ourselves, not God. By our natural birth we have no future, because we are separated from God. God does not throw us out. Instead He offers us a new birth. He offers to remake us, so we can again serve Him. Like the milk-carton-turned-flowerpot, the sinner-turned-Christian has a new reason for living.

There are several important things to remember about this new birth. First of all, you cannot make yourself be born again. Birth is something that's *given* to us. Our second birth is caused by the power of Christ in our hearts. Jesus tells us that it comes by the water and the Spirit. This is the gift of Baptism, by which Christ gives us a new life. In another part of the Bible, Baptism is called a "washing of regeneration," a washing that brings rebirth. Through the Word of God in Baptism, the Holy Spirit brings Christ to us as our Savior. He gives us the life of Christ as our new life.

Also, remember that your new life in Christ gives you a new reason for living. You will still have your old life, so there will always be a struggle. But the new life is the one that will last forever. Christ's death has taken care of the problem of our first nature. It is His resurrection that gives us the new life. We do not have to wait until we are in heaven to have that new life. It is given to us now, that we might now live with God, that we might now serve Him.

Read the Instructions First

The Word

And he [the rich man] said: "Then I beg you, father, to send him [Lazarus] to my father's house, for I have five brothers, so that he may warn them, lest they also come into this place of torment." But Abraham said: "They have Moses and the prophets; let them hear them." And he said: "No, father Abraham; but if someone goes to them from the dead, they will repent." He said to him: "If they do not hear Moses and the prophets, neither will they be convinced if someone should rise from the dead." Luke 16:27-31 (from the Gospel for the First Sunday After Trinity)

The World

A plastic model not assembled, a tube of glue.

Suppose you were putting together a model like this and lost the glue that came with the kit. Since you liked the model, you went out and bought another tube of glue. But when you used the new glue, it wouldn't stick the pieces together. Instead it caused the pieces to melt and twist out of shape. That ruined your whole model.

You might take the glue back to the store where you bought it and ask the manager for a new model, since the glue you bought from him ruined yours. But the manager would say: "I'm sorry; you just didn't read the directions. See, it says right on the tube, 'Do not use on plastic.' Did you read what it said?"

You might try to defend yourself by saying that the warning should have been printed in bigger letters or in red letters, or the clerk should have mentioned it to you when you bought it. But none of those defenses would work. The fact is, you just did not read the instructions.

Jesus' parable about Lazarus and the rich man tells about a man who had not read the instructions. The rich man had ignored the Word of God. When he died, he went to hell. Then he asked that someone go back to warn his brothers. But he is told that they can read Moses and the prophets, that is, the Bible, which shows the way of salvation. The rich man knew that he had not read the Bible and that his brothers wouldn't either; so he suggests that if someone rose from the dead they might believe him. But he is told that if they won't believe the Bible they would also find a reason for not believing someone from the dead.

This parable tells us to learn God's plan of salvation in Christ. The Bible tells you that God has given you salvation through Christ. Perhaps the rich man did not want to read the Bible because he would have read that he had to feed and help the beggar Lazarus at his gate.

When you read how Christ has saved you, you will also read that He has saved you for a purpose. He will tell you to share what you have with the poor. He will tell you to love people of other races. He will tell you to be kind to those that hurt you. But do not avoid the Scriptures because they tell you to do such difficult things. It is the Christ who has saved you who tells you to do them. By the same power with which He saved you from your sin He will also help you serve Him by loving others. He will use you to do for others what He has already done for you.

Make Your Choice

The Word

But they all alike began to make excuses. The first said to him: "I have bought a field, and I must go out and see it; I pray you, have me excused." And another said: "I have bought five yoke of oxen, and I go to examine them; I pray you, have me excused." And another said: "I have married a wife, and therefore I cannot come." Luke 14:18-20 (from the Gospel for the Second Sunday After Trinity)

The World

Two birthday invitations (see messages below).

Aren't you happy when the mail comes and there's a letter for you? Here's one for you now. It says: "Please come to my birthday party next Wednesday at 3 p. m. Your cousin, Tom." I am sure you'll enjoy the party. Look! Here's another letter for you. It says: "What: a party. Where: at my house. When: Wednesday at 3 p. m. Who: your friend Amy."

Now you have a problem. You are glad to get both invitations, but why do they have to be for parties at the same time? Maybe this has never happened to you; but if it did, you would have to make a choice. You could go to only one party or the other.

The people in our text also had to make a choice. The text is part of a parable Jesus told. A man had invited many of his friends to dinner. One man had a choice between going to the dinner and looking at a new farm he had recently bought. He looked at the farm. Another man had a choice between the dinner and seeing if he had gotten a good deal on some oxen. He checked the oxen. Another had a choice between the dinner and staying home with his wife. He stayed home. In each case those who made the choice showed what was most important to them.

Jesus tells us this parable because we also make choices daily. When you decide between playing a game or watching TV, you show which is more important to you. When you choose between going to church and Sunday school or going on a picnic, you show which is more important to you.

But the choice Jesus asks you to make in this parable is more than just whether or not you'll go to church one Sunday or read a chapter of the Bible a day. He asks you to make a choice about the whole purpose of your life. Everybody wants to live with God forever. If that were the choice, it would be simple. It sounds great to go to heaven and be with God when you die.

But do you want to live with Him now? That is the choice Jesus is asking you to face. Do you want to live with Him now and accept His way of life as your way of life? Will you let His friends be your friends? Will you share in the work Christ has given to all who follow Him?

Before you make the choice, remember the choice that Christ has already made. He has chosen you. It was His choice that He come to earth to become your Savior. He has given His love to you by giving His life for you. He has accepted you as His own. His choice rejects no one and accepts everyone. Aren't you glad He made that choice? Think about it before you make your own.

Who Is the Most Important?

The Word

Or what woman, having ten silver coins, if she loses one coin, does not light a lamp and sweep the house and seek diligently until she finds it? And when she has found it, she calls together her friends and neighbors, saying, "Rejoice with me, for I have found the coin which I had lost." Just so, I tell you, there is joy before the angels of God over one sinner who repents. Luke 15:8-10 (from the Gospel for the Third Sunday After Trinity)

The World

Two large cards: one with the numerals 1, 2, 3, 4, 5; the other the same except that "3" is omitted, with an obvious space showing the omission.

Who do you think is the most important person to God? It might seem that there is no answer to such a question, because God loves all people. Christ came to die for all people. God does not play favorites.

Yet Jesus uses a story to show how some people are more important in a given situation. He tells of a woman who lost a coin. The lost coin became the most important, so she searched until she found it. Maybe we could understand this by looking at this card with the numbers 1, 2, 3, 4, 5 on it.

I am going to ask each of you to pick a number. Have you picked one? Why did you choose that number? Everyone who chose a number did so for a different reason. If your birthday is on one of the first five days of a month, you may have picked that number. You may have chosen the number in your family. Anyway, each of the numbers was probably selected by someone.

But now look at this card (card with numeral 3 omitted).

Now when I ask you to think of a number from 1 to 5, all of you will think of the same number. The number 3 has become the most important, but not because it has been written larger than the others or written in a different color. It is the most important because it is not there. The number 3 belongs between 2 and 4, but it is not there. When we looked at the card that had all the numbers, we chose many different ones. But looking at the card with a number omitted made us all think of the missing number.

So it is that Jesus says the most important person to God is the one who has not received the love that God has for all people. He is the most important, but not because God loves Him more. It is because God loves everyone that the one who has rejected His love becomes most important. All people belong with God. God made us all. Christ died for us all. We belong with God. The ones who are not with Him are missed.

This does not mean that if you want God's attention you leave Him so He will come looking for you. You have God's attention or you would not be with Him. To say that those who have rejected God are the most important does not say that you are less important. He knows you are with Him when you receive the love that Christ gives you. He does not forget those who are with Him while He searches for those who have rejected Him.

This parable does mean that you also are to be concerned about those who have rejected God. A coin can't look for coins, but people can look for people. You can tell others about the love of Christ. You can tell others why they belong with Christ. God does His looking for others through us.

You Can't Give Until You Get

The Word

Why do you see the speck that is in your brother's eye, but do not notice the log that is in your own eye? Or how can you say to your brother, "Brother, let me take out the speck that is in your eye," when you yourself do not see the log that is in your own eye? You hypocrite, first take the log out of your own eye, and then you will see clearly to take out the speck that is in your brother's eye. Luke 6:41-42 (from the Gospel for the Fourth Sunday After Trinity)

The World

A white dinner plate with a small black smudge (shoe polish) in the middle; a cloth that has several heavy spots of shoe polish.

When your family has company for dinner, you can help your mother by setting the table. As you are putting the plates on the table, you notice that one has a spot on it. (Show plate.) It would be embarrassing for company to sit down to dinner and have a dirty plate. So you take a cloth to wipe the plate clean. (Hold up the plate and wipe so additional polish is rubbed on the plate.)

This is not helping, is it? Instead of the plate getting cleaner, it is becoming even dirtier. You can see why. The cloth is also dirty. You cannot clean a dirty plate with a dirty cloth. First the cloth would have to be cleaned; then it could be used to clean the plate.

Jesus says that you and I can be like that dirty cloth. The cloth did more harm than good in cleaning the plate. We do more harm than good when we condemn other people's sins. When you see someone else's fault and tell everyone about it, you are not removing the sin. You are only adding your sin to the other person's by spreading it around. When you complain that others are not being good Christians, you are not helping them become good Christians. You are only showing that you also are not a good Christian.

We cannot correct another person's sin, because we also are sinners. When we talk about their sin, we are only adding our sins to theirs—like the dirty cloth adding more dirt to the plate. Jesus says: "Why do you see the speck that is in your brother's eye, but do not notice the log that is in your own eye?"

That does not mean that we can just ignore sin. But it does mean that before we can help someone else we must first find an answer to our own sin. Before the cloth could clean the plate, the cloth had to be cleaned.

The answer to your sin is that Christ has paid for your guilt. The Bible says: "The blood of Jesus Christ, His Son, cleanses us from all sin." Jesus says: "You hypocrite, first take the log out of your own eye, and then you will see clearly to take out the speck that is in your brother's eye." The word *hypocrite* was for those who wanted to help fight other people's sin but ignored their own. If you recognize your sin, you can do as Jesus said. First receive forgiveness for your own sin. Then help your brother with his sin. You can give him help that really helps. You don't just tell him that he is wrong. Instead you can tell him how he can be made right. Tell him about the forgiveness that Christ offers to all people. Tell him how it is possible to be forgiven. Tell him how you know that your own sins are forgiven.

Don't add to the burden of sin by condemning it. Anybody can be against sin. But Christ did more than be against sin. He paid for it. Now we can also do something about it. We can share His forgiveness with those who need it.

Don't Forget the Lure

The Word

Jesus said to Simon: "Do not be afraid; henceforth you will be catching men." And when they had brought their boats to land, they left everything and followed Him." Luke 5:10-11 (from the Gospel for the Fifth Sunday After Trinity)

The World

Fishing gear including rod, reel, line, creel; however, only one lure, which is not attached to the line.

Jesus told His disciples to become fishers of men. They had been fishermen, but they had always caught fish. Yet they left their boats filled with the greatest catch of fish they had ever seen to go out to catch men.

We still talk about being fishers of men. Few if any of us have ever been full-time fishermen as the disciples had been. To us fishing is a hobby, something to do on vacation. Maybe this is why we aren't better fishers of men — we think of it only as a hobby or as a part-time occupation. But Jesus made it a full-time occupation for all Christians. Ministers and missionaries are not the only fishers of men. We all are. And I would like to give you a lesson on being a fisher of men.

This is fishing gear — not the kind that the disciples used. They used nets. But this gear can show us something important about fishing for men. This is a good rod and reel — the kind successful fishermen use. It has a strong line so the fish won't get away once it is caught. Here is a creel to hold the fish after they are caught. Looks like I am ready to go fishing.

But have you noticed? I left out the most important part of the equipment. I could have all this fishing gear and couldn't possibly catch a fish. I also need this (lure). Without this to attract the fish and its hook to catch the fish, all the rest of the equipment is useless. The rod and reel can help get the lure to the right spot. The line and creel can keep the fish after it is caught. But only the lure can do the catching.

We also have a lot of equipment as fishers of men. We have buildings and organs, classes and programs, tracts and Bibles. We sponsor radio and TV programs. We support schools and missionaries. We have all those things that are necessary to operate a church. But unless we have a lure to attract and catch men, we can never be fishers of men.

That lure is the Gospel of Jesus Christ. It is the message that Christ is the Savior of all mankind. The buildings and the programs can help us get that message to the right spot. The music and the lessons can help keep a person with the church. But it is only the Gospel of Christ that can save a man.

We have nothing else to offer people — nothing but God's love and mercy in Jesus Christ; nothing but forgiveness, not just in words but in our attitudes toward others. We can be fishers of men only by showing Christ in our lives by our words and our actions.

How Good Do I Have to Be?

For I tell you, unless your righteousness exceeds that of the scribes and Pharisees, you will never enter the kingdom of heaven. Matthew 5:20 (from the Gospel for the Sixth Sunday After Trinity)

The World

Two balloons (shaped like watermelons, not like French bread), a scissors, a needle.

How good do I have to be to go to heaven? Jesus answers by saying that one must be better than the scribes and Pharisees. The scribes and Pharisees were very good people. They had strict moral laws, and they followed those laws down to the last letter. Yet Jesus says that we have to be better than they to enter the kingdom of heaven. I am going to show you something with these two balloons that might help you understand how good you have to be to go to heaven.

First, I cut the end off this balloon with a scissors. Now I will try to blow it up. Of course you know it won't work. The balloon can't be blown up, because the air goes right through it. This balloon is no good.

Let this balloon be an example of one who knows that he has not been good enough to go to heaven. Anyone who is aware of his sins knows that he cannot earn a place in heaven. That would be as impossible as blowing up a balloon that had the end cut off.

Now look at another balloon. I am going to poke just a little hole in this balloon. (Use needle to puncture the balloon about half an inch from its opening. Make sure the needle goes through both sides.) You can't even see that little hole. If you hadn't seen me make the hole, you would never know it was there.

Let this balloon be an example of a person who has not committed big and open sins. We all say such a person is a good person. His faults are so small that no one can see them. He may even forget about them himself because everyone else's sins are much more obvious. But look at what happens when I blow this balloon up. (Blow up the balloon. It will break before it is full blown.) Now this balloon is no better than the one that had the end cut off. Neither one can be blown up. One had a huge hole, one had only a tiny hole. Yet neither passed the test of usage.

If you ask how big a hole a balloon can have in it and still be good, the answer is, None at all. If you ask how many sins a person can commit and still earn heaven, the answer is, None at all. If you want to earn heaven, you cannot just be good, you cannot just be better than other people. You must be *perfect*.

Christ has been perfect for you. He lived without a single sin, and He lived for you. He died to pay for your sins. He has earned heaven for you. You cannot and you need not earn it for yourself. Whether your sins are open and obvious to all, or whether they are secret and known only to yourself, Christ has died for you. You can go to heaven. But you will go not because you are good but because Christ is good. That's how good He had to be.

You Can Afford to Care

The Word

[Jesus said,] "I have compassion on the crowd, because they have been with Me now three days and have nothing to eat." . . . And He commanded the crowd to sit down on the ground; and He took the seven loaves, and having given thanks He broke them and gave them to His disciples to set before the people; and they set them before the crowd. And they had a few small fish; and having blessed them, He commanded that these also should be set before them. And they ate and were satisfied; and they took up the broken pieces left over, seven baskets full. And there were about four thousand people. Mark 8:2, 6-9 (from the Gospel for the Seventh Sunday After Trinity)

The World

A paper sack containing a large bottle of catsup and a small, single-serving container of catsup (like those received at drive-ins).

Suppose that you are on a cookout with a dozen of your friends. Each of you has your own sack of food, and you are all cooking hot dogs over the fire. You hear the others asking one another if they brought along any catsup, and you hear the disappointed replies saying they have none.

Then you look in your sack and find this (small container of catsup). You know that it is not enough for everyone; so you have to pretend that you don't know that they want catsup. To keep from being selfish you could give it to one of your friends, but which one? Because you don't have enough to share with everyone, you can't share with anyone. If you would have found this in your sack (big bottle of catsup), you could have afforded to notice that all your friends wanted catsup, because you would have had enough for everyone.

91

In today's text there were 4,000 hungry people. Many of them must have realized that others were also hungry. But they couldn't afford to say anything about it, because they couldn't do anything about it. Only Jesus could afford to have compassion on the crowd. He saw their hunger and was concerned. He wasn't afraid to be concerned, because He could do something about it. He took the little food they had, a few loaves of bread and a couple of fish, and invited everyone to sit down to eat. Imagine inviting 4,000 people to dinner when all you have is a few loaves of bread and a few fish. But Jesus had more than that. He had the power of God, which He used to multiply the bread and fish into enough to feed 4,000 people and even have seven baskets of leftovers.

From this let us learn two things. First, Jesus is not afraid to see our needs, because He can do something about those needs. He does not ignore our sin; He forgives it. He does not shut His eyes to our problems. He shares in them by being with us. Jesus does not have to stay away from us because He does not want to see us suffer. He knows that He will give us victory over suffering.

Second, we also can afford to see the needs of others. By ourselves we are often afraid to see how hungry others are, how sick they are, how lonely they are. We wonder what we can do about it. Remember that we are a part of the church, the body of Christ. I am not alone. You are not alone. We are united with Christ. Together with Him we can face the needs of people. Together we can feed more than 4,000 people. Together we can show concern for the lonely and sick. Let us always be aware that we are together, together with one another and together with Christ. We can afford to care, because we have Him with us.

Watch What You Eat

The Word

Beware of false prophets, who come to you in sheep's clothing but inwardly are ravenous wolves. You will know them by their fruits. Are grapes gathered from thorns, or figs from thistles? Matthew 7:15-16 (from the Gospel for the Eighth Sunday After Trinity)

The World

A graham cracker; a can of pressurized shaving cream that has been encased in a tube of paper on which is printed in large letters, *whipped cream.*

Are you generally hungry when you come home from playing? Most children are. As you go home, you might hope for a piece of cake or some cookies. But suppose no one is home when you arrive. You look around for something to eat and all you find is graham crackers. Graham crackers are okay, but you had been counting on something better. Maybe you can dress the graham cracker up a bit. In the refrigerator you find this can. Whipped cream should make the cracker better. So you spread a generous amount on the cracker. That should be delicious.

It should be, but I can tell you that it is not. I won't ask one of you children to eat this cracker, because I don't want to make you sick. But look! (Remove paper from the can.) This isn't whipped cream. It's shaving cream. The cracker with the shaving cream may look good, but it would taste terrible. Not only would you be disappointed by not having cracker and whipped cream, but the cracker is now also ruined. The lesson is: Be careful what you put on your food; you might ruin it.

The purpose of that lesson is to help you understand a much more important lesson. Jesus said: "Beware of false prophets, who come to you in sheep's clothing but inwardly are ravenous wolves." Just as we become hungry for something to eat, we also have a need for spiritual food. We need to know that God cares for us and is with us. We receive this spiritual food by listening to prophets—those who speak the message of God. But we must be careful not to listen to false prophets. Just as the shaving cream looked like whipped cream, so also messages that do not come from God may sound like they are from God.

Just because there are false prophets does not mean that you should avoid all prophets. You must learn which message is from God and which is not. You recognize good food by its taste. You recognize true prophets by what their teaching does for you and others.

A prophet must teach all of God's Word. He cannot leave out the Law and still be a prophet. You must hear the Law to know what God expects of you and how you have failed. You need to hear the Law so you know you cannot depend on yourself but instead must turn to God for help.

A true prophet must also show that God has given you help. If you had only the Law, you would not be receiving all of God's Word. God also tells you that He has sent His Son to be your Savior. The message that Christ has come to remove the guilt of your sin tells you that you do not have to be afraid of God. It tells you that you can be near Him now and forever. The fruit, or results, of such a message from God is that you have salvation.

Beware of false prophets. Beware—that is, avoid—any message that makes you either trust in yourself or be afraid of God. But look for the message that helps you admit all your faults before God and yet know the love God has given you through Christ.

How to Be on the Winning Team

The Word

And I tell you, make friends for yourselves by means of unrighteous mammon, so that when it fails they may receive you into the eternal habitations. Luke 16:9 (from the Gospel for the Ninth Sunday After Trinity)

The World

A chalkboard on which is drawn a baseball scoreboard with teams listed as "Visitors" and "Home," chalk.

Today's text follows the story of a business manager who is fired by his boss because he has wasted the boss's property. The manager wanted another job; so he made friends with his boss's creditors by reducing the amount they owed. What he did was wrong, but to the manager's surprise the boss said: "You did the smart thing. You lost this job because you were dishonest; you might as well be dishonest all the way, so other dishonest people will hire you."

In telling this parable Jesus didn't mean to praise the manager's dishonesty — only his cleverness. God wants us to be smart. He does not want us to pull a foolish stunt like the one I'm going to describe now.

Pretend you're at a ball game. Here is the scoreboard. You are for the home team and are seated on their side of the park. During the first inning the visitors score two runs, the home team none. (Mark score.) The second inning gives the visitors another run, the home team none. (Mark score.) When the visitors score three in the third inning, you become discouraged, especially after the home team fails even to get on base. (Mark score.) You sit glumly through the next three innings as neither team scores. (Mark score.)

It looks as if your team has lost—unless you change teams. By moving over to the other side of the ball park it would be easy to be on the winning side, you figure. So you move over. You sit with the visitors and cheer for them. After you have moved, you cheer through the seventh and eighth innings, as neither side scores. (Mark score.) During the top half of the last inning the visitors, who are now your team, score nothing. (Mark score.) Three more outs and the game is won! But the home team goes to bat and makes seven runs. The game is over! The team you deserted has won. By changing teams you ended up on the losing side. You weren't smart like the dishonest business manager. You were very foolish.

So also in life we want to be on the winning side, and that's God's side. But God's side often looks like the losing side. Christians are humble instead of proud. Christians see the needs of others and share with them. Christians love people of other races. Christians love those who hate them.

Sometimes it seems easier to switch sides, to do what the world wants you to do rather than what Christ would do through you. But don't switch sides until you've thought about the whole ball game. The last inning of your life will be your death. The world tries to ignore the last inning. The world never wants to talk about who is going to win the game of life. It only wants to talk about who is ahead now.

But Christ was willing to lose the innings—He was laughed at, He served others rather than Himself, He died. But He won the ball game. He rose from the dead. He made the only run that wins forever. Only when you are on His team can you face the last inning. Play not to be ahead but to win.

It's a Crying Shame

The Word

And when He drew near and saw the city, He wept over it, saying, "Would that even today you knew the things that make for peace! But now they are hid from your eyes." Luke 19:41-42 (from the Gospel for the Tenth Sunday After Trinity)

The World

A child, a roll of fine wire, a wire cutter.

When Jesus came to Jerusalem, He stopped outside the city and cried. He cried because He saw something in the city that hurt Him. Let's picture this by having someone help me. Jerry, will you stand up here near me? You will have to stand still, because I'm going to wrap this wire around your ankles. (Wind wire tightly around ankles.) This wire is thin, but it is strong. If Jerry tried to pull himself out of it, it would cut his legs; so be careful, Jerry. The wire is now wound together in such a way that Jerry cannot get himself free. If he tries, he will hurt himself.

That is a sad sight. If you thought of him being tied up somewhere all alone, you might cry as you thought how afraid he would be. Jesus saw the people of Jerusalem all tied up in their sins. He saw how they had ignored God's Word, which told them to prepare for a Messiah. He saw how they were proud and depended on themselves instead of God. He saw their greed and how they refused to help one another. And Jesus cried. He cried because He loved the people of Jerusalem and He did not like to see their suffering.

Would Jesus cry if He saw us in our sins? Are we tied up and alone, with no way out? He does love us. Does He have to weep over us because of that love? To answer, let us look at another reason He cried over Jerusalem.

He said: "Would that even today you knew the things that make for peace." It was sad that the people had problems, but even sadder that there was help which they refused. He came to bring an answer to the sin that tied them up, but they refused Him. Imagine Jerry all tied up in that wire — with this wire cutter right beside him. But suppose he refused to use it. Then it would be sad not only that he was tied up but that he refused the help that was there.

Jesus does not have to cry over our sins, because He has taken them away by His death for us. But when we refuse the forgiveness He offers, we are being like the people of Jerusalem or like the boy who refused to use a wire cutter to free himself. It is easy to refuse forgiveness. It is easy to pretend we don't need it. It is easy to feel so sorry for ourselves that we think no one will help us. It is easy to be so comfortable with sin that we don't want to give it up. Christ said that the way of peace was hidden from those in Jerusalem. It becomes hidden from us when we refuse it in the way it is given.

The message of peace can be hidden from you if you forget that you need it or choose to ignore it. But look at what it offers you. Just as this wire cutter will release Jerry from this wire (cut wire loose), so also the gift of Christ will free you from the chains of sin. It's a crying shame to have help and not use it. It's a crying shame that there is a Savior who forgives all sin and yet many refuse His forgiveness. But instead of crying, let's receive the help that Christ gives.

Life Is an Open Book

The Word

I tell you, this man went down to his house justified rather than the other; for everyone who exalts himself will be humbled, but he who humbles himself will be exalted. Luke 18:14 (from the Gospel for the Eleventh Sunday After Trinity)

The World

A book that can be destroyed; a roll of cellophane tape.

Jesus told a story of how two men used their religion. Both went to the temple. One used the opportunity to think and talk about how good he was. He thanked God for all the good things he had done and reminded God of all the bad things he had not done.

The other man used the same opportunity to think and talk about how bad he was. He stood alone and said, "God, be merciful to me a sinner!" Jesus then said: "I tell you, this man went down to his house justified rather than the other." Then Jesus applied the story to all of us by adding, "For everyone who exalts himself will be humbled, but he who humbles himself will be exalted."

To understand what "exalting" and "humbling" ourselves mean, let's compare our lives to this book. The book is now complete; it is in good condition. Our lives were meant to be good. We are the children of God. But we have sinned and destroyed the goodness of our lives. Sin has done to us what it does to this book when I tear some of the pages. (Tear out several pages, leaving stubs long enough so the torn section can be taped back in.) When the pages are torn out, the book loses its value. The loose pages could be lost or put into the wrong place. It would be difficult to read the book now.

The book still looks fine from the outside. If I carefully stick these torn pages inside the book, no one could tell that it has been damaged. See, the book looks just the same as before the pages were torn. If someone came along with a roll of tape and offered to repair any torn books I had, I would have two choices. I could say: "This book doesn't need repairing. See how good it is? It looks great." As long as I kept the book closed, no one would know the difference. But then the book wouldn't be repaired.

My second choice would be to open the book and say: "This book has torn pages. Will you fix it?" Then the torn pages could be taped back in. (Do it.) In this case I would have had to admit that the book was torn, but at least it would be repaired.

Your life is like the book. Sin has destroyed your goodness. Christ comes along, like the person with the roll of tape, and asks if He can help you. You have two choices. You can keep your life to yourself—like a closed book. You can say: "See, I am good. I have done many good things. There are many bad things that I haven't done."

Your other choice is to open your life and let Christ see all your sins. He can repair your life, because He lived for you. He gave His life to pay for your sins. When you admit your sins to Him, you have admitted that you are not perfect. But you are also letting Him give you His perfection.

Let your life be an open book before Christ.

Wait for the Whole Story

The Word

[Jesus] sighed, and said to him: "Ephphatha," that is, "Be opened." And his ears were opened, his tongue was released, and he spoke plainly. And He charged them to tell no one; but the more He charged them, the more zealously they proclaimed it. And they were astonished beyond measure, saying: "He has done all things well; He even makes the deaf hear and the dumb speak." Mark 7:34-37 (from the Gospel for the Twelfth Sunday After Trinity)

The World

A child's billfold with a secret compartment containing a $10 bill.

All of you know that you are supposed to tell others about Jesus. But listen to what the text for today says. First, Jesus healed a deaf man. After the man could hear, the first thing Jesus told him was that he should not tell anyone about the miracle. How strange! It seems that Jesus should have told him to tell others. The man was excited about having his hearing. After years of being deaf he was anxious to hear everyone's voice. So, despite what Jesus had told him, the man told everyone how Jesus had healed him. All the people who heard were amazed and said, "[Jesus] does all things well; He even makes the deaf hear and the dumb speak."

Jesus had a reason for telling this man not to tell other people about the miracle. The man knew only part of the story. He didn't know all that there was to tell. We could compare it to your receiving this billfold as a gift.

Suppose your father gave you the billfold and said: "This is a special gift, and I want you to take care of it. Let me show you how. . . ." But you are so excited about the billfold that you interrupt him by saying, "I know how to take care of it. I won't lose it. Honest." Then you are so anxious to show the gift to your friends that you run out the door and leave your father standing there. He had something else to say to you. He wanted to show you this secret pocket, which contains a $10 bill. But you were so excited about the billfold that you never stayed to hear the whole story. You told your friends about the billfold, but you didn't know about the $10 hidden in it.

That's what happened to the man in the text. He was so glad to have his hearing restored that he never stayed around to find out that Jesus could do much more than cure his deafness. Jesus could forgive His sins. Jesus could have given him eternal life. If the man would have listened to Jesus, he would have had an even more important message to tell his friends, because it would have been for them too.

You should also learn all of the story about Jesus. He is more than someone to be with you in the dark. He is more than someone to help you when you are sick. He is more than someone who loves you when others don't seem to. Jesus is all of those things, but He is also your Savior. He helps you in many ways, but His greatest help to you is that He has taken away your guilt.

Do not use this story as a reason for not telling others about Jesus. But use it to remind yourself and others of the real reason why Jesus is so important in your life. He has done something for you that no one else could ever do. He has given you eternal life.

I Didn't Do Anything Wrong

The Word

"Which of these three, do you think, proved neighbor to the man who fell among the robbers?" He said, "The one who showed mercy on him." And Jesus said to him: "Go and do likewise." Luke 10:36-37 (from the Gospel for the Thirteenth Sunday After Trinity)

The World

A carton of milk that has been opened and reclosed; a large, flat pan.

Watch something that happens in many homes where there are children. An opened carton of milk is on the table. One child walks by and accidentally knocks the milk over. At home milk would be spilled all over the table and floor. To have a limited mess here, I am going to tip the milk carton over in this big pan. Let's suppose that your sister was the one who knocked it over. But you are sitting right beside it. Because the carton has been reclosed, the milk doesn't all spill out immediately. It slowly gurgles out as you sit beside it and watch.

If your mother walked in, she would probably yell at you. You could defend yourself by saying: "I didn't do anything wrong. Sister knocked it over. I didn't touch it." But I doubt that your mother would accept that defense. She might say: "You didn't do anything right either. You should have picked the carton up so the milk wouldn't run all over everything."

The story of the spilled milk might help you understand Jesus' parable of the Good Samaritan. The priest and the Levite didn't do anything wrong. It was the robber who had hurt the man and almost killed him. Yet the priest and the

Levite didn't do anything right either. They ignored the man who was injured. They knew he needed help, but they didn't want to get involved. They were like you when you sat beside the milk and watched it gurgle out on the floor. They were guilty because they had done nothing. But the Good Samaritan was willing to help. He gave his time and money to help the man who had been injured. He gave love in the way Christ gives love. And Jesus tells us to do the same.

You and I can be guilty if we ignore other people who need our help. In your school there will be children who are lonely and need someone to say hello to them. Will you ignore them? There are people in our community who are hungry and who need better clothing. Are you going to pretend that you don't know about them? There are people living near you who are different from you—different race, different religion, different ideas about how to live. Are you willing to be a neighbor to them?

Remember that Christ has not only forgiven your sins when you have done wrong but He has also forgiven you when you have not done anything right. Use His forgiveness to change your life. He has given you love, not because you deserve it but because He wants to give it. You now have that kind of love to give to others. Don't be afraid to love those who need it.

Receive the Gift and the Giver

The Word

"Was no one found to return and give praise to God except this for-
eigner?" And He said to him: "Rise and go your way; your faith has
made you well." Luke 17:18-19 (from the Gospel for the Fourteenth
Sunday After Trinity)

The World

An envelope containing a letter and a dollar bill; another dollar bill.

When Jesus healed ten lepers, nine of them were so glad
to be healed that they rushed home to enjoy a normal life
again. One of them was so glad Jesus healed him that he
came back to thank Jesus. All ten were healed, but only to
the one who gave thanks did Jesus say: "Rise and go your
way; your faith has made you well." They all received the
same gift; yet there seems to be a difference in those gifts.
Let's compare this to a kind of gift that you are more used
to receiving.

You receive a letter in the mail from your grandmother.
When you open it, you find not only the letter she wrote you
but also a dollar bill. That is a nice gift. You can use the
dollar for many things.

On the same day, as you are walking along the sidewalk,
you glance down and find a dollar. Since it is not in a billfold,
there is no way of telling who lost it. So you have another
dollar.

The dollar you found and the dollar your grandmother
gave you are worth exactly the same — one hundred pennies.
Each will buy the same thing. But one has a much greater

personal value than the other. The dollar you found was an accident — a bit of luck, if you wish to call it that. It means only that you now have a dollar to spend. You may never find another dollar on the sidewalk the rest of your life.

But the dollar your grandmother gave you has much more value. In the first place, it was not luck that gave it to you but love. The gift showed that your grandmother thought about you and wanted to share something with you. You received not only the dollar, which you could spend, but you also received the gift as a sign of your grandmother's love. In the second place, your grandmother will continue to love you. While you may not find another dollar, your grandmother will probably give you more gifts. Another difference, which may be a responsibility, is that you have no one to thank for the dollar you found. But you will write to your grandmother to thank her for the gift she sent. Though the two dollars look the same, one has much more meaning for you.

So also with the ten cured lepers. Nine received only healing from a sickness. To them it was a single gift, an important one, the only one they thought about. But the tenth leper received the same healing and in addition received the Christ who gave the healing. He received not only a gift but also the Giver. He had someone to thank.

How about you? Do you accept the gifts of God as something you find on a sidewalk? Do you regard the good things of life as pieces of luck, or do you regard them as blessings? God has more to give you than health, family, and home. He has sent His Son to be your Savior. Christ has forgiven your sins so that you can enjoy all His blessings now and forever. Enjoy His gifts, but also enjoy the Giver.

Don't Follow "Shortcut" Religion

The Word

But seek first His kingdom and His righteousness, and all these things shall be yours as well. Matthew 6:33 (from the Gospel for the Fifteenth Sunday After Trinity)

The World

A chalkboard, chalk, eraser.

I am going to give you an arithmetic assignment. (Write four addition problems on the board, involving two-figure numbers.) For most of you these problems are simple, but remember that at some time you had to learn how to do them. So you also pretend that they are difficult now.

There are two ways you could look at this assignment. We'll call the first way the "shortcut" way. If your goal is to get an A in arithmetic, the shortest way to an A is to ask someone else for the answers. If you asked the right person, he could give you the answers easily. (Write the answers in quickly.) Of course, that would be cheating. The A in arithmetic would also be false, for you wouldn't have gotten from your lessons what they were supposed to teach you. When someday you really have to add numbers, you wouldn't know how to do it.

The other method would be to work on the problems. (Erase answers.) Working out the answer by yourself would take more time, and you might be wrong on some, but you would be learning how to add. (Work answers out as one is learning.) This method might not give you an A, but you would be able to add numbers and go on to more difficult number work.

There is also a shortcut approach to religion. If the purpose of your religion is to make yourself look good, you can do it by building your own image. You can pretend that you are a good person. You can work hard and save money to have wealth and prestige, and people will look up to you.

Jesus warns us against shortcut religion when He says: "Seek first [God's] kingdom and His righteousness, and all these things shall be yours as well." Shortcut religion may make a person look good, but it will not do what religion is supposed to do for you. It will not bring you close to God. It will only make you think that you do not need God or that you have brought yourself to God.

Jesus says that we should instead seek God's kingdom. The purpose of life should be not to live for ourselves but to live for Him. To be a part of His kingdom we also need His righteousness, that is, His goodness. We cannot depend on our own good works. We cannot claim that we are good enough to be with Him. The way to God's kingdom is the way of the Cross. It shows us that Christ died for us to give us His righteousness. It shows that we come to God by the Cross as we repent of our sins and receive the grace that Christ gives.

Jesus tells us that if we first of all have God's kingdom and His righteousness, we will have other things as well. We can enjoy the good things of life, but let's not get them by taking a shortcut that leaves God out. The purpose of life is not to *look* good but rather to *be* good. We can be good only by receiving the goodness of Christ. There is no shortcut.

Choose Your Lifesaver

The Word

[Jesus] said: "Young man, I say to you, arise." And the dead man sat up and began to speak. And He gave him to his mother. Luke 7:14-15 (from the Gospel for the Sixteenth Sunday After Trinity)

The World

A dollar bill, a bottle of medicine, a picture of a family, a cross — all in a box.

In this box are four lifesavers. Each one is a symbol of something many people use as a lifesaver. I am going to explain each one to you and ask you to choose the lifesaver you want.

The first is a dollar bill. Of course, one dollar won't save you, but it is used as a symbol for all money. Money could save your life many times. If you were hungry, it would buy food. If you were cold, it would buy clothing and a place to live. If you were in a dangerous place, it would buy you a ride to safety.

There are two problems in using money as a lifesaver. The first and less important is that you can't spend more than you have. The second and more important is that there are things that it can't buy. If there is no food, money will do no good. The same is true of everything that you normally buy with money. Then there are some things that can't be bought with money. One of them is life itself. Money may, in some cases, be a life-prolonger, but it is not a lifesaver, because those with money die just as regularly as those without.

Another lifesaver: a bottle of medicine. Again, it is a symbol for all the medical devices available to us. The lives of many of us have been saved by operations, vaccinations, or drugs. In each of these cases our lives were saved for awhile. Again the medicine is a life-prolonger rather than a lifesaver. Even the healthy people eventually die.

This picture, the third of our lifesavers, is a symbol for family and friends — the ones who love you. They are lifesavers because they give you a reason for living and because they would do anything they could for you. They would help you receive medical attention. They would give you money when you need it. Some loved ones would even risk their life to save yours. But they still can't save your life every time you need a lifesaver. There will be a time when they will have to say helplessly: "Isn't there something that can be done?" And the doctor will have to say hopelessly: "No."

The cross is the fourth of our symbols of lifesavers. It reminds us that Christ died for us and that He rose from the dead. He had already shown that His victory over death was not just a personal victory for Him. It was a victory He shared with all people. He proved that even before His death by showing His power over death. In our text He told a dead man to arise. The man did. He was restored to the kind of life he had had before. He was to die again. But someday the young man in the text will arise again, this time (assuming he became a believer) to a new life that will never end. You and I will share in that new life. *Christ is the only lifesaver without limitations.*

We will use all the life-prolongers God has given. We are grateful for our life on this earth, because Christ lives with us now. He is the Lifesaver who will take us from this life to an even greater life in heaven. He has chosen to be our Lifesaver.

Be Yourself

The Word

But when you are invited, go and sit in the lowest place, so that when your host comes he may say to you, "Friend, go up higher"; then you will be honored in the presence of all who sit at table with you. For everyone who exalts himself will be humbled, and he who humbles himself will be exalted. Luke 14:10-11 (from the Gospel for the Seventeenth Sunday After Trinity)

The World

Two marbles, the same size, one of which has been placed in a deflated balloon; a pin.

Jesus recognized that all people like to pretend to be more important than they really are. We like to try to impress each other by making others think that we are very smart, very rich, very good looking, or very good. Jesus tells us that it is wrong for us to puff ourselves up by pretending to be something that we are not.

Maybe we can understand the dangers of pride by comparing ourselves to this marble. The size of the marble will represent your total ability. It is your intelligence, appearance, wealth, talent, moral behavior all rolled into one little ball the size of this marble. But you don't like others to see the small size of your collected abilities, so you put the marble in a balloon, as I have this one. Now I can blow up the balloon with the marble inside. (Do it.) Now people can't see how little the marble is. They see the big balloon and are much impressed by the size of your collected abilities.

There is a problem, however. Inside, you know that you are faking. You still feel like the little marble, but now you are rolling around in the big balloon (shake it), trying to keep up appearances. Others may see you and be impressed, but you will be uncomfortable with yourself. Worse yet, someone will challenge all that ability you have been bragging about and — bang! (break balloon) — your image is gone. People see how small you really are. (Hold up the marble.) That is what Jesus meant when He said: "Everyone who exalts himself will be humbled."

But Jesus also tells us something else. We do not have to be ashamed to be ourselves, even though our talents, intelligence, wealth, and the like are much less than those of others. Even though we know we are very limited in many ways, God loves us for what we are. You do not have to pretend to be something that you are not. God knew what you were when He sent Christ to be your Savior. Christ has forgiven your sins. You are a child of God.

You still have reasons for being humble. All you have that is good comes from the grace of God through Christ. But with His power you can use whatever intelligence you have for a good purpose. The purpose will not be to puff yourself up but to serve God and man on this earth. You can use your wealth, your personality, your talents. You don't have to pretend to have more than you have, but you can be honest in using all that God has given you to its full extent.

Jesus also promised: "He who humbles himself will be exalted." When you recognize your own limitations but do not give up, when you use every talent God has given you to His glory, you will also be exalted. You will share the exaltation of Christ, who has won a victory for you. Find out who you are by finding the Savior who loves you as you are and who will change you to be like Him.

Look at Both Sides

The Word

Now while the Pharisees were gathered together, Jesus asked them a question, saying: "What do you think of the Christ? Whose Son is He?" They said to Him, "The Son of David." He said to them: "How is it then that David, inspired by the Spirit, calls Him Lord, saying: 'The Lord said to my Lord, Sit at My right hand, till I put Thy enemies under Thy feet'? If David thus calls Him Lord, how is He his Son?" Matthew 22:41-45 (from the Gospel for the Eighteenth Sunday After Trinity)

The World

A large cardboard of a different color on either side (perhaps the top of a fancy box), in this case gold and white. Any colors will do.

Think carefully before you answer this question to yourself. What color is this cardboard? (Show gold side.) Look at it carefully. If you answered, "Gold," you are not completely right. If you said, "Gold on one side," you were correct. (Turn cardboard.) See, the other side is white. The point is that you gave an answer with only half the evidence.

The same thing happened to the Pharisees in the text. They were discussing the Messiah with Jesus. We know that Jesus is the Messiah, but the Pharisees had refused to believe Him though they had seen His miracles and heard His teaching. They knew the Old Testament passages that tell about the coming Messiah. Jesus asked them whose son the Messiah would be. This is an important question, since the Old Testament identifies the Messiah by His nation, tribe, and family. The Pharisees answered correctly: "The son of David." The Messiah was to be born of the family of King David. Many prophecies had said so. Jesus could have pointed out to them that both His mother and foster father were from the family of David.

Instead Jesus quotes another Old Testament passage regarding the Messiah which the Pharisees also knew. In Psalm 110 David was speaking about the Messiah and called the Messiah his Lord. If the Messiah were to be the son of David, that means one of his descendants, how could David call Him Lord? The Pharisees believed that the Messiah had not yet come, but David spoke of Him as though He had existed a thousand years before their time.

The Pharisees could not answer Jesus' question, because this did not fit into their idea of what the Messiah would be. But they were looking at only one side of the picture. They were right. The Messiah was the son of David. But He was also the Son of God. He existed long before David, and He was David's Lord just as He is our Lord today. As this card is both gold and white, so the Messiah was to be both God and man. He was always the Son of God; He became the Son of Man when He was born of Mary in Bethlehem.

Always remember both sides of the life of Christ. If God seems distant and far away, remember that Christ became human and lives with us. He is a part of your human existence. But when you have doubts about your salvation, when you wonder if you really have had help from God, turn the card over. Remember that He is also true God. Remember that He rules heaven and earth. Remember that He is the One on whom your salvation depends.

Never let Christ become only one or the other, God or man, in your life. Remember that He is always both God and man for you.

You Can Check the Power

The Word

"For which is easier, to say, 'Your sins are forgiven,' or to say, 'Rise and walk'? But that you may know that the Son of Man has authority on earth to forgive sins" — He then said to the paralytic — "Rise, take up your bed, and go home." And he rose and went home. Matthew 9:5-7 (from the Gospel for the Nineteenth Sunday After Trinity)

The World

An extension cord (plugged into a source of power), two hairpins, a small lamp.

Several men brought their paralyzed friend to Jesus. Jesus looked at the man and said: "Your sins are forgiven." The man's outward appearance did not change any. We don't look any different after our sins are forgiven. Those who heard Jesus did not believe that He could forgive sins. In fact, they accused Him of blasphemy. For any man to claim that he is God is blasphemy. Only God can forgive sins; so it would be blasphemy for a man to claim the power to forgive sins. They doubted Jesus' power and challenged it.

To understand that we also doubt power when we cannot see it work, look at this extension cord. You cannot tell by looking at it whether it is connected to the power of electricity. We could find out easily. I have two hairpins. If I would put a hairpin in each side of the socket on the extension cord and if any of you would come up and touch both points at the same time, we would find out. If the extension cord works, you would get quite a shock.

But there is a better way to check the cord. I'll plug this lamp into the socket. See, the lamp works; so there is power in the cord. Actually, it takes very little power to light this lamp. But because that small amount of power is there, we also know that there is more power available — enough to really shock someone.

Jesus also proved His power to forgive sins by using His power in a lesser way. He said to the paralytic: "Rise, take up your bed, and go home." And the man did it. You can't argue against that kind of power. The power to forgive is not visible. But the power to heal a man either shows or it doesn't work. Those who objected to Jesus forgiving sins had no more to say. They couldn't argue against something they had seen.

We know that Christ has the power to forgive sins. That power does not have to be proved each time He gives us forgiveness. The power of His forgiveness is shown by His dying for us. We know His payment was complete because He rose again from the dead. His death and resurrection assure us of His power to forgive sins. When the guilt of our sins is taken away by Christ, we too can look forward to a resurrection from the dead. We know that God's power to forgive us is not limited. It is a power that has been tested by death itself.

Accept the Invitation You Receive

The Word

Then he said to his servants: "The wedding is ready, but those invited were not worthy. Go therefore to the thoroughfares, and invite to the marriage feast as many as you find." And those servants went out into the streets and gathered all whom they found, both bad and good; so the wedding hall was filled with guests. . . . For many are called, but few are chosen. Matthew 22:8-10, 14 (from the Gospel for the Twentieth Sunday After Trinity)

The World

An invitation and a card (messages below).

Suppose you received an invitation that said (read from invitation): "Please come to my house for a cookout Friday evening at 6:30." You surely would not send back a reply like this (read from card): "I am sorry I cannot come Friday evening, but I will come Saturday at 12:30. Since I do not like cookouts, I would rather have a more formal dinner in your dining room."

I hope that none of you would be so bold as to change an invitation. You cannot receive an invitation and change it to suit yourself. Yet in one of His parables Jesus tells us about people who did just that. Some of them couldn't come at the time the host had invited them. Others just said they didn't want to come. Another came but refused to wear the wedding garment the host had provided. In the parable the host then sends his servants out to find other people to come to the party. He invites poor people, the crippled, the blind, and many others who were not normally invited to parties. But they came and had a great time. Then Jesus ends the parable by saying: "For many are called, but few are chosen."

Jesus told this parable to teach us how we are called to be with Him. Jesus has invited everyone. He died for all. He has said: "Come unto Me, all who are weak and heavy laden, and I will give you rest." He has said that in His Father's house there are many places and that He is going to prepare a place for us. We are all called to be with Christ, but He has also said, "Few are chosen." Does that mean that maybe we won't get to heaven even though we have been invited? It does not say that we will be refused. But it does say that we might refuse the invitation. We might try to change it to suit ourselves.

Your invitation to eternal life is given in the name of Christ, God's Son, who is your Savior. To accept the invitation you must accept it in Christ's name. To deny Christ is to deny the way the invitation was given.

Your invitation from God is for all people. If you want to limit it only to those whom you like, you are changing the invitation. If you refuse to love other people and to receive their love, you are changing the invitation. You are saying that you do not want to associate with those whom God loves. In the parable the host invited those whom society had rejected, and he rejected those who thought they were better than others. God also will reject those who reject the ones He loves.

Your invitation is for now. The invitation to be with Christ is not for just the day you die. Thank God, it *is* for that day; but it is also for *today* and for *every day* in between. The invitation cannot be ignored or put off until you have more time to think about it.

Remember that God has called you. He has chosen you in Christ to be His child. Are you willing to take the invitation as He gives it?

Whom Can You Trust?

The Word

Jesus therefore said to him: "Unless you see signs and wonders, you will not believe." The official said to him: "Sir, come down before my child dies." Jesus said to him: "Go; your son will live." The man believed the word that Jesus spoke to him and went his way. John 4:48-50 (from the Gospel for the Twenty-first Sunday After Trinity)

The World

A child, money (the local price of a child's ticket to a movie), a ticket hidden someplace in the room where the child can be directed to find it.

Some people say: "I won't believe anything that I can't see. I have to have proof." I hope you are not a person who believes only what he sees. Our text tells us that we should believe without having to see proof. To show you why this is important, I will ask Sue to come and help me.

Sue, pretend you are a person who will not believe what you cannot see. I tell you that I am going to buy you a ticket for the movies. But you won't believe it until you see it; so here, I give you the money to buy the ticket. Only after you have the money will you get ready to go to the theater.

Now let's try again. Instead of giving you the money, I tell you that the ticket is waiting for you at the theater. Now you have a choice to make. If you don't believe me, you won't go to the movie, because you can't see the ticket. Or if you believe me, you will have to get ready and go before you have seen proof. Pretend that the pulpit over there is the theater. You go over there. The ticket is under the book. See, the ticket is there. If you had not believed what you had not seen, you would not have gone to look for it. You have to believe many things you cannot see.

In the text the man asked that Jesus heal his child. Jesus asked him if he believed only because he saw miracles. The man said that he already believed. It was because he believed that he asked for a miracle. Jesus then told him that his son was well. But remember that the child was back home. If the man really believed Jesus, he could go on home. If he had to have proof before he believed, he would have asked for that proof. But the man showed his faith in Christ by going home without proof. When he arrived, the son was well.

You know about God by faith, not by sight. If all that you could know about God was what you could learn through your sight and understanding, then God's love for you would be limited by your ability to understand it and accept it. But faith helps us accept things about God that are far beyond our normal understanding. *God loves you.* Maybe you can't see why. But accept it by faith! *Christ died for you.* It isn't necessary for you to have been on Calvary to know that His death took away your guilt. It is by faith that you receive this. *Christ rose from the dead.* You have not seen His resurrected body, but it is by faith that you know He lives today in you.

Faith comes to us by the power of the Holy Spirit through the message of the Gospel. Receive the Word and let the Holy Spirit give you the faith.

The Forgiven Are Forgiving

The Word

"Then his lord summoned him and said to him, 'You wicked servant! I forgave you all that debt because you besought me; and should not you have had mercy on your fellow servant, as I had mercy on you?'" Matthew 18:32-33 (from the Gospel for the Twenty-second Sunday After Trinity)

The World

A child's coin bank and a handful of coins.

The text is the conclusion of a parable Jesus told about forgiveness. A servant owed his master a big debt, which he could not pay. The master could have thrown the servant into prison. Instead he forgave the servant the debt. Then the servant went out and found another servant who owed him a small debt. The second servant asked for more time to pay the debt. But the first servant refused. He had the second servant thrown into jail. When the master heard about that, he was angry and said, "You wicked servant! I forgave you all that debt because you besought me; and should not you have had mercy on your fellow servant, as I had mercy on you?"

This parable tells us that we who have forgiveness can give forgiveness. Many times it is difficult to forgive other people when they hurt us. Sometimes other people keep on hurting us, and we feel that we have run out of forgiveness to give. But Jesus tells us a way to keep on giving forgiveness. We will see how He helps us by using an illustration.

121

Suppose this is your bank, like the bank you may have at home to keep your money in. Also, suppose that you owe your friend a dime. The friend comes to ask you for the dime. But (shake the bank) the bank is empty. You can't pay your debt. You have no money. You have to tell your friend that you can't pay him.

However, your father hears you tell your friend that you can't pay him. So your father reaches into his pocket and pulls out a handful of coins, which he puts into the bank (put coins in bank). Now (shake the bank) you can pay your friend. Not only can you give him the dime you owe him but you have other money left in the bank.

To understand the illustration, let the coins remind you of forgiveness. You owe other people forgiveness. You have to forgive the brother or sister who used your toys without asking you. You must forgive the bully at school who called you bad names. Sometimes you must even forgive your parents. But it is difficult to forgive. Often your heart may feel like the bank — empty. You have no forgiveness.

When you feel that way, remember that your Father in heaven sees your need. He gives you forgiveness. He sent His Son, Christ, to die for your sins. He has forgiven you for everything you have done wrong. He has forgiven the words you have said to hurt others. He even forgives bad thoughts. There is no limit to the forgiveness He gives. It is like the handful of coins — given without being counted.

If you have received His forgiveness, you have forgiveness to give to others. You can forgive others because Christ has forgiven you. Anytime you think you cannot forgive, remember how much forgiveness Christ has given to you. Use that forgiveness to share with others.

Where Does Your Money Go?

The Word

[Jesus] said to them: "Render therefore to Caesar the things that are Caesar's, and to God the things that are God's." Matthew 22:21 (from the Gospel for the Twenty-third Sunday After Trinity)

The World

A box (cigar box or equivalent size) divided into four sections, which are labeled "Savings," "Church," "Spending," "Gifts"; two cards (size of the box), with "My Money" printed on one and "What God Has Given Me" printed on the other; a quarter and five nickels.

Some people once came to Jesus with a question they thought He couldn't answer. They weren't interested in an answer. All they wanted was to give Him some trouble. The question was: "Is it lawful to pay taxes to Caesar?" Jesus answered: "Render therefore to Caesar the things that are Caesar's, and to God the things that are God's." This is more than a clever answer to avoid being for or against the Roman government of that day. The answer makes us think about how we use our money. Do I spend part of it on myself and give some to God? Or is God involved in the way I spend all my money?

To apply this to your life, we will use this box as a place where you keep your money. See, it has four sections: "Savings," "Church," "Spending," "Gifts." The idea is that when you receive money you put it into one of these sections.

When you receive a quarter you have to decide where to put it in your money box. You could divide the quarter into change. Here are five nickels. Let's see, I'll put one nickel for "savings," one for "church," one for "spending," one for "gifts" — that is to buy presents for members of your family for birthdays or Christmas. But there is one nickel left. I could divide it into five pennies and put one into each section. But I would still have a penny left. Maybe I should put the whole nickel into "spending." There are many things I'd like to buy. Or should it go into "savings"? Maybe I'll need it later. Since Christmas is coming, maybe it should go into "gifts." No, since I am a Christian, it should go into the "Church" section. Or should it?

Do you think that the money I put into the "Church" section goes to God, and the rest is for me? Is it not also a part of my Christian faith that I have some in "savings," as long as I do not trust in them? Am I being less Christian if I spend some money on myself from the "spending" section? Shouldn't I share with others by buying "gifts"?

More important than dividing the money is the label I put on the box. Do I put this label on it ("My Money")? Or this one ("What God Has Given Me")?

If I put the first label on the box, I am only using a part of my money as though it came from God. I am putting God into one corner of life. But if I use the second label, and mean it, then all my money is being used in a Christian way. Christ is the Savior of all of your life — not just one little section called "Church." Use your Christian faith when you save money. Use it when you spend money. Use it when you give money.

Your life cannot be divided up into sections labeled "For God," "Against God," and "Without God." Christ gave His total life for you. He is with you always — not just on Sunday mornings or when you are good. Let your faith in Christ help you in all that you do.

How to Do a Miracle

The Word

A ruler came in and knelt before Him, saying: "My daughter has just died; but come and lay Your hand on her, and she will live." And Jesus rose and followed Him, with His disciples. And behold, a woman who had suffered from a hemorrhage for twelve years came up behind Him and touched the fringe of His garment; for she said to herself: "If I only touch His garment, I shall be made well." Matthew 9:18-21 (from the Gospel for the Twenty-fourth Sunday After Trinity)

The World

A necktie.

The easiest way to learn how to do something is to watch someone who knows how. For example, have you boys learned how to tie a necktie yet? Maybe you girls should know how, too. You might be able to use this knot for a belt or a band around your neck. I could go into a long description of how to tie the necktie. But it is easier for me to show you. Watch. After you watched me tie it a couple of times you would be ready to do it.

Do you think that if we watched Jesus do several miracles, we could learn to perform miracles too? In the text we hear two people say how they think a miracle should be done. A man whose daughter had just died comes to Jesus and asks for help. He says: "Lay your hand on her, and she will live." He had heard how Jesus had laid His hands on others to heal them. He was sure that if Jesus did the same thing for his daughter, she would be raised from the dead.

As Jesus went to the man's home to do as the man had asked, a woman who was ill came near Him. She also wanted a miracle from Jesus. She said to herself: "If I only touch His garment, I shall be made well." She had a different idea of how a miracle should be performed.

Think of other ways Jesus performed miracles. Sometimes He spoke to the person who was sick. He even spoke to Lazarus, who was dead. Yet the dead man responded to His words. In one case Jesus spit in some dust and made clay, which He put on a blind man's eyes. Another time He stuck His fingers into a deaf man's ears. Sometimes He performed miracles of healing without even going near the person who was ill.

That Jesus performed miracles in so many ways shows us one thing—we can't learn to do miracles by watching Him, then trying to do the same thing. To learn to do miracles is not like learning to tie a necktie. The secret of Jesus' miracles is not the *way* He did them but *who* did them. He was God living among men. He had the power of God, which He used to help people in many different needs.

The age of miracles is not past. But we must see that Christ has come to us in our own time and place. He is here by the power of His Word, which we study and know. Today's miracles are spiritual ones. When an unbeliever is brought to faith, that's the greatest miracle of all. The miracle of conversion was going on already when Christ was on earth, but since Pentecost God has made this miracle happen much more often than before.

To turn God's power off and on to impress people is not the great miracle. Jesus never did it that way. The great miracle is that God's power is still at work; missionaries are preaching the Gospel, and many people are coming to faith. The great miracle is that you and I have also come to faith and know the love of Christ.

Treasure in a Junkpile

The Word

Let him who is on the housetop not go down to take what is in his house; and let him who is in the field not turn back to take his mantle. Matthew 24:17-18 (from the Gospel for the Twenty-fifth Sunday After Trinity)

The World

An assortment of items that might be left on the street for the trashman when a family moves (old toys, paper-towel holder, cooking utensils, etc.); a new football.

When a family moves away, they sometimes leave a pile of junk for the trashman to pick up. Suppose you were looking through the stack before the trashman came. You might find all kinds of interesting and usable things — like this paper-towel holder (pick it up) or some old toys that could be fixed up almost as good as new (add them to your hand); or this pan could come in handy (add it to what you hold). Before long your hands would be full — like mine are right now. But you keep on looking. If you found something worthwhile, you would also find a way to carry it.

Then you spot something that makes you drop everything. (Put down the junk and pick up the football.) Look, a brand-new football! You don't try to keep the old junk and the football too. The football is so great that you've forgotten all about the rest. You can't wait to tell the gang about this.

Now let's compare Judgment Day to finding the football. We live in a world that has many interesting things to do. There is excitement and challenge in every day of our life. All we have to do is look for it and recognize it — like finding worthwhile things in a junkpile. But there will come a time when the earth will be destroyed. We call it Judgment Day. That day will come when we don't expect it. It will find us busy with many things to do. Our hands will be full, like mine were with all that junk I held. Then Christ will come and show us the new life He has prepared for us.

What will you do? Will you want to keep the life you already have? Will you think about all the good things you have on earth and hesitate to leave them? In our text Jesus tells us that we should not turn back for anything on earth. He says: "Let him who is on the housetop not go down to take what is in his house; and let him who is in the field not turn back to take his mantle." When Judgment Day comes we can drop everything on this earth, because we have seen something new and better. I don't like to compare this life to living in a junkpile, but when we see what God offers us in eternity the comparison fits.

Jesus does not tell you to sit around and do nothing until Judgment Day. Enjoy the life He has given you now. But always remember that Judgment Day is a part of Christ's Good News. It is not a day to take away the joys we now have. It is a day on which we will receive even greater joys from God.

Because Christ has already come to be our Savior, we do not dread His coming to be our Judge. Be ready for His coming. Be ready to drop everything and welcome Him.

Jesus in Everyday Life

The Word

"I was hungry and you gave Me food, I was thirsty and you gave Me drink, I was a stranger and you welcomed Me, I was naked and you clothed Me, I was sick and you visited Me, I was in prison and you came to Me." Then the righteous will answer Him: "Lord, when did we see Thee hungry and feed Thee, or thirsty and give Thee drink? And when did we see Thee a stranger and welcome Thee, or naked and clothe Thee? And when did we see Thee sick or in prison and visit Thee?" And the King will answer them: "Truly, I say to you, as you did it to one of the least of these My brethren, you did it to Me." Matthew 25:35-40 (from the Gospel for the Twenty-sixth Sunday After Trinity)

The World

Clipboard, two pieces of paper (different colors), carbon paper, ball-point pen.

It is difficult to think of anything to give Jesus, because He has everything. Yet in our text He tells us that we can give Him food, water, clothing, and that we can visit Him when He is sick and lonely. He says that we can give these things to Him by giving them to those people who need food, water, clothing, or who need to be visited because they are sick and lonely. So we have no excuse for not giving to Jesus. There are many, many people who are in need, and we can give to Him by giving to them.

The problem is that it is difficult for us to understand how we can be giving something to Jesus by giving it to someone else. None of us would fail to give to Jesus if He were in need, but we do fail to give to others who are in need. Maybe this sheet of paper will help. (Hold up clipboard

129

with one sheet of paper on it.) Do you know that I can write my name on this paper without touching it with a pen or a pencil or anything else that writes? I'll show you how. (Add carbon paper and the other sheet of paper to the clipboard.) Now I will write my name on this yellow paper. Remember, the paper I said I would write my name on without touching was white. I have not touched the white paper. But look at it! My name is written on it.

That was not magic—it was carbon paper. Anyone can do it. And it is not magic when, in giving food to a hungry person, you have given it to Christ even though you have not seen Him. I was able to write on one paper and have it show up on the other because they were connected, in a way, by the carbon paper. So Christ is connected with all people. He is connected with every human being by virtue of His birth as a true human being. He is connected with us by His suffering for us, His death for us, and His resurrection for us. His life, like the carbon paper, transferred His goodness to us. It gives us His victory over death.

Now, the carbon paper also works the other way. Anything we Christians do for others is done for Him—even though we do not actually see Him. It is true even though the other person does not believe in Him, since He still loves that person. Anytime you see anybody in need, you have an opportunity to help Christ by helping that person. This does not mean that you use a person only as a tool by which you help Christ. It is because Christ loves you and you love Him that you can love that person too.

As you live with people, remember Jesus' words: "Truly, I say to you, as you did it to one of the least of these My brethren, you did it to Me."

When Will You Get Ready?

The Word

Afterward the other maidens came also, saying: "Lord, lord, open to us." But he replied: "Truly, I say to you, I do not know you." Watch therefore, for you know neither the day nor the hour. Matthew 25:11-13 (from the Gospel for the Last Sunday After Trinity)

The World

A lunch pail, and a box containing thermos bottle, sandwiches, cookies, fruit, or other items that would be packed for lunch.

The text is a conclusion to a parable Jesus told about ten young ladies who were invited to a wedding party. The wedding was at night, but none of them knew what time. Five of the ladies kept a lamp with oil ready, so they could see to go to the party when it started. The other five used up their oil. When the party started, the last five had to run to a store to get oil to have light. By the time they came back, the party had started and they were excluded.

Jesus tells us that His parable shows us how we should be ready for Judgment Day. Do you know when to get ready for Judgment Day? Maybe this illustration will help. Suppose one of your friends invites you to go on a Saturday outing with him. You are supposed to pack your lunch and be ready when he stops by to pick you up. There are two different times when you could get ready.

You might wait until your friend comes and then start packing your lunch. (Open pail and start putting things in.) But it takes time to pack a lunch. It might take longer than your friend could wait. Your other choice would be to pack the lunch ahead of time. (Finish packing the lunch and close the pail.) Then you would have it all packed and ready when your friend comes.

We know that there will be a Judgment Day, when Christ will return to earth and all the dead will be raised. There are two times when you could get ready for Judgment Day. You might try to wait until it happens and then start to get ready. When Judgment Day comes, everyone will know about Jesus. Everyone will then know that the most important thing in life is to be ready for eternity. But then it will be too late to get ready for eternity, because you will already be in it. Like the five young ladies without oil, or like you if you wait to pack the lunch after your friend arrives, it is too late.

We are told to be prepared now. The five wise ladies prepared for the party by having oil. You prepared for your friend by having the lunch ready when he came. You prepared for heaven by seeing your guilt now and recognizing that you do not deserve heaven. Then you also see that Christ has come to earth to forgive all your guilt. You are prepared when you know that He is your Savior who has died for you. When He comes, you will not have to be afraid. You will not have to wonder, "What shall I do?" You will know that He has already done everything for you by saving you.

You are prepared when you have faith in Christ. Make this faith a part of your daily life.